J.-K. Huysmans

a reference guide

A
Reference
Publication
in
Literature

Marilyn Gaull
Editor

J.-K. Huysmans

a reference guide

G.A. CEVASCO

G.K. HALL & CO.

70 LINCOLN STREET, BOSTON, MASS.

539375

PQ
2309
.H4
Z9935
1980

Library of Congress Cataloging in Publication Data

Cevasco, George A
   J.-K. Huysmans: a reference guide.

   (A Reference guide in literature)
   Includes index.
   1. Huysmans, Joris Karl, 1848-1907–Bibliography.
I. Series: Reference guide in literature.
Z8430.55.C39   [PQ2309.H4]   016.843'8
ISBN 0-8161-8235-3   79-22426

This publication is printed on permanent/durable acid-free paper
MANUFACTURED IN THE UNITED STATES OF AMERICA

Contents

Introduction

When Joris-Karl Huysmans published A Rebours in Paris during May of 1884, he claimed that he had written it for only a few close friends. The book, however, became a sensation, which amazed everyone, especially Huysmans. While Emile Zola, his friend and mentor, feared that A Rebours would undermine Naturalism, others were annoyed and indignant.

Huysmans was viewed as a misanthropic impressionist; his fictional hero, a lunatic of a complex sort. One critic was kind enough to advise the novelist he ought to allow himself to be confined in a hydropathic establishment for a short spell. Extremes of criticism echoing around Paris helped the book become an instant best-seller. More important than any momentary appeal was the novel's impact on the psychology of a whole generation, not only in France, but in England as well. A Rebours soon became, in the memorable words of Arthur Symons, "the Breviary of the Decadence" (1893.2; this citation and others that follow are to works listed under the appropriate year in Part II of this Guide).

Symons could have labelled A Rebours a primer or a guide, a manual or a textbook, a compilation or a miscellany, or even an anthology; for all such terms are descriptive of Huysmans' novel. "Breviary," however, struck Symons as the exact word, aware that a breviary is a special prayer book of psalms, hymns, and selected parts of Holy Scripture read daily by ordained clergymen of the Roman Catholic Church. A Rebours, he also knew, was a breviary of sorts, its scripture being one of art, music, flowers, gems, and liqueurs that aesthetes--men who consecrated their lives to a religion of beauty--read day in and day out.

Des Esseintes, Huysmans' bizarre hero in A Rebours, became the dandy of the day. A character whose complex make-up had elements of Comte de Montesquiou-Fesenzac, Baudelaire, Barbey d'Aurevilly, Flaubert, and Huysmans himself, Des Esseintes' influence knew no bounds. Both an obviously derived figure and yet an essentially original creation, at once the legatee of Romantic and Naturalistic heroes and

the prototype of those who were to follow in Decadent and Symbolist
literature (1933.5), Des Esseintes soon became the literary rage of
France and England.

In France, A Rebours broke the formula that Zola and the Naturalists had imposed on the novel (1884.1). Poets began to compose under
the shadow of Des Esseintes and to sing paeans of praise for Huysmans. Mallarmé dedicated one of his longest and most interesting
poems, "Prose pour Des Esseintes," to Huysmans. Lorraine offered his
"Nevrose pour Karl-Joris [sic] Huysmans." Poems found in Adore Flou-
pette's Les Deliquescences were obviously inspired by A Rebours.
Dozens of other writers who also felt that literature had to emerge
from the pit of Naturalism into which it had so abysmally sunk found
new hope in Huysmans' novel.

In England, Des Esseintes captured the fancy of young writers re-
ceptive to what was being written on the other side of the Channel.
Almost in reaction to the Victorian condemnation of French literature
as gross, cynical, and immoral, these men of letters adulated and
emulated Des Esseintes and his mode of life (1960.8).

Oscar Wilde, for one, fell under the spell of Des Esseintes.
Huysmans' hero particularly influenced Wilde's Dorian Gray. A true
Decadent, Dorian possessed nine copies of Huysmans' "Poisonous Book,"
each bound in a different color to suit his various moods and the
changing fancies of his nature, over which, like most Decadents, he
had slowly lost control. Wilde often maintained that no one can
really be corrupted by a book, but his Dorian is. The influence of
A Rebours on Wilde's own private life is imponderable.

In 1895, at the notorious Queensberry trial, when the prosecutor
for the Crown, Edward Carson, cross-examined Wilde as to the identity
of this same French novel, Wilde identified it readily enough as
Huysmans' A Rebours. Requested to say something about the novel's
morality or immorality, Wilde refused. To ask a writer to pass moral
judgment on a fellow writer's work, he protested, would be an impertinence and a vulgarity. Carson harped on Huysmans' A Rebours because he too wondered about its influence on Wilde, especially since
the author of Dorian Gray gave the impression that he was so over-
whelmed by the aesthetic sensationalism found in Huysmans' novel that
he remained insensitive to the spiritual dilemma it contains
(1975.7).

But what was there about A Rebours that so captivated Wilde and
influenced the entire Decadent Movement? All of Huysmans' previous
works had proclaimed that life was worthless, indeed; but now he had
evolved one central theme: for a privileged few there might be art.
And Huysmans had written a novel about an aesthete who had but one
purpose in life--the pursuit of pure beauty. Decadents fed on art
insatiably, and A Rebours fascinated them because they read it as a
monograph on aesthetic neurasthenia, as a breviary that treated all
the senses to a complete course in overwhelming voluptuousness. To

model oneself on the spectacular career of Des Esseintes, moreover,
became obligatory for all young artists who sought kinship with the
Decadent elite (1970.15).

At the turn of the century, after the Decadent Movement expired,
interest in A Rebours waned, but the novel survived the Nineties and
continued to be read, no longer as a "breviary" but as an exotic
piece of literature. Enthusiasm was strained and sporadic at times,
but A Rebours could not be laid aside. The novel was destined for
more than a single literary period, and for more than a limited number of aesthetes in France and England. Almost a century has now
passed since A Rebours was first published, and interest in the work
is holding fast.

In the Twenties, Huysmans' name began to appear in important
critical studies of French literature; by the Thirties, he was acknowledged a significant figure among the writers of the world. In-
ternationally, his life, his books, and his influence are being
studied with a scholarly zest. In Germany and Italy, Huysmans has
had so many translators, critics, and devotees, their names would
fill a small book. In Denmark, one of the country's leading men of
letters, Johannes Jorgensen, early came under Huysmans' influence,
and his Autobiography contains several references to his literary
idol. In the Netherlands, Huysmans' foremost devotee, translator,
and critic is Jan G. Siebelinck. In Spain, Vicente Blasco-Ibañez
has been one of Huysmans' better translators; in Argentina, Juan B.
Gonzalez.

Although Huysmans has never been a favorite with the French reading public, his reputation in France is firmly established. All lit-
erate Parisians know him, of course, if not as an outstanding literary artist, at least as a writer famous enough to have a street
commemorate his name. Rue Huysmans, however, is by no means an important artery. Smaller than Avenue Emile Zola, Boulevard Voltaire,
Avenue Hugo, and Boulevard Diderot, for example, it gives some indi-
cation to the ordinary Parisian of Huysmans' position among French
authors. Better informed Frenchmen know of the existence of the
Société Huysmans.

The Société originated in 1919, when several of the author's
friends and admirers came together twelve years after his death to
found a literary club in his memory. The Société is still active
today; and since 1928, it has published the informative Bulletin de
la Société J.-K. Huysmans, a biannual journal. Far from being a
seedy charitable association, such as one finds in France, patiently
trying to fan the embers of some dying reputation, the Société J.-K.
Huysmans is a flourishing literary organization that numbers among
its members several prominent, internationally-known scholars.

To weigh quantitatively the literary reputation of Huysmans,
nonetheless, might be tantamount to reducing him to failure. His
books have never filtered down to any but a select group of readers

throughout the world. But Huysmans never sought popular appeal; indeed, he condemned the writer who wrote with one eye on his manuscript and the other on a cash register. Devotion to literary art was his prime vocation, and everything he wrote was a consequence of his aesthetic dedication. In his unique fashion, Huysmans was an extraordinary artist and innovator. What he lacked as a novelist was the ability to develop his characters with the power of a Balzac; nor did he have the subtlety of a Flaubert. Dumas' command of adventure and Hugo's romantic trappings are also missing from Huysmans' fiction. What he did have was an unparalleled genius for presenting in words whatever he felt or experienced. In his analysis of ill-defined states of emotion he is superb, and to some extent he anticipated Marcel Proust.

Among English men of letters--if any parallel can be drawn--Huysmans somewhat resembles Walter Pater. Both had an ornamental and somewhat flamboyant manner of expression, and both often sacrificed rhythmic variety and tone to color. As prose stylists, their phrases were always crystal clear and sonorous. Like Pater, Huysmans enriched the world with the elaboration of aesthetics; but unlike his English counterpart, Huysmans was frequently guilty of a brutal coarseness, especially in his earlier novels in which he dwelt on decidedly unpleasant physical ailments and sexual matters from which the master of English prose would have shrunk with horror. Their paths never crossed, but had they met they could have run on for days in their fervor for art.

Pater delighted in French art and literature, in the culture of a country he frequently maintained was superior to his own. A dedicated Francophile, Pater was nevertheless troubled by his impression of Paris as a remarkable city populated with an exuberant crop of eccentrics. In art, in literature, in politics, and in philosophy, they held center stage (1973.11). From Pater's point of view, never were so many absurd doctrines preached. The outlook, he knew, was far from encouraging for most of these young intellectuals, and the Franco-Prussian War had contributed to their pessimism. Positivism held sway, but there was little faith in progress and humanity. For the dogmas of religion, the intelligentsia substituted creeds of economic determinism. Darwinism and theories of heredity and environment were deified.

Artists and writers, for the most part, were at loggerheads when it came to democracy, universal suffrage, socialism or any social change; but they seemed united in their campaign against conservatism and clericalism. Content mostly with thought and concerned little with action, they shunned responsibility, questioned free will, derided idealism, and scoffed at religion. Man, they rationalized while they sipped their absinthe and smoked their hashish, as they read Schopenhauer and Marx, had too much of the beast in him. What could be done in this heyday of materialism? Gone was the spiritual zeal of the Middle Ages. There was no impetus of a Renaissance. Echoes of Comte, Taine, Renan filled the air (1971.7).

Introduction

What can be specified among all such generalizations is that as an important representative of his time and culture, as a child of his age, Huysmans wrote books that serve as texts in which one may actually experience the intellectual and spiritual mores of the fin de siècle. Having had an uncanny insight into the late nineteenth-century mind, his works accurately recorded most of the important thoughts of the period.

His first work was a volume of prose poems, Le Drageoir à épices. Marthe, a story of a Parisian prostitute, was his first novel. Next followed Les Soeurs Vatard, a dismal novel of two working girls and their lovers; then En Ménage, a study of the disenchantment of married life; and then A Vau-l'Eau, a sordid history of a poor, lame, discontented, middle-aged bachelor. During this phase of Naturalism, Huysmans also wrote "Sac au dos," a short story on the disgusting barbarity of the Franco-Prussian War, which he contributed to Les Soirées de Médan, a notorious collection of short stories written by Zola and his group (1928.4). During his naturalistic period Huysmans also developed an interest in art, and Croquis parisiens and L'Art moderne contain his first aesthetic critiques.

By the time Naturalism went out of fashion around the mid-eighties and curiosity about the mystic and the occult began to stimulate the Parisian literary world, Huysmans had already turned to the impressionistic and the symbolical. The foremost work of his second period is, of course, that veritable Bible of the Decadents, A Rebours. En Rade, a novel of the grotesque realities of rural life, followed. Un Dilemme, a prolonged anecdote of an abandoned girl; Certains, a volume of art criticism; La Bièvre, a record of certain impressions he received in his wanderings about the older sections of Paris; and Là-Bas, his infamous novel of diabolism, were also written during his second period.

En Route is the first novel of a trilogy written during his final period. This mostly autobiographical work is the story of a weary Parisian writer eager for something pure and true in which to believe. The personality of the author is kept distinct from his fictional counterpart, but essentially the process of spiritual conversion remains the same. Drawn by liturgical art, the main character envisions the Church as a hospital for sick souls. La Cathédrale and L'Oblat complete the trilogy, giving one of the fullest and most penetrating studies of conversion to be found in literature (1964.1). All three novels are primarily concerned with the searchings and fluctuations of Huysmans' soul as he travels the road toward spiritual peace.

La Cathédrale is a study of Chartres containing pages packed with learning, objective detail, and mystic symbolism. L'Oblat, a novel of mysticism, covers the period of Huysmans' novitiate as a Benedictine Oblate and his forced return to Paris when religious orders were expelled from France by the anti-clerical laws of 1901. Along with his biography Sainte Lydwine and his book on Les Foules de Lourdes, his famous trilogy is distinguished by a violent realism and sensuous indelicacy not found in ordinary, colorless Catholic literature.

From 1874 to 1894, the period in which Huysmans wrote his naturalistic and decadent works, his novels were not translated into other languages. After the publication of En Route in 1895, his reputation slowly began to spread to England and America. Some five years before, Stuart Merrill, the Franco-American poet, first translated Bourget, Mallarmé, Mendes, and Huysmans, presenting them in a little volume of prose-poems entitled Pastels in Prose. Prefaced by W. D. Howells, who was also fascinated by Continental writers, the book contained but one pinch out of Huysmans' spice box. From Le Drageoir à épices Merrill chose "Red Cameo"; but it was a pinch that aroused little interest.

After the publication of " Red Cameo" (or as Merrill preferred, "Camaieu in Red") there was no further translation of Huysmans into English until 1896. Possibly it was felt that much of the French author's power over words would be lost; yet when translations were finally attempted, most retained enough to make the ventures worthwhile. During the next few years, many more translators and critics began to find their way to Huysmans (1933.2).

Before the turn of the century, translations of En Route and La Cathédrale were undertaken in England by Kegan Paul. Huysmans' death in 1907 drew attention to these works in particular, but no other translations were published. Interest in translating Huysmans declined in both England and America during the decade from 1908 to 1918. In 1919, an American edition of En Route appeared, followed by The Cathedral in 1922, St. Lydwine in 1924, and The Oblate and The Crowds of Lourdes in 1925.

Huysmans' two most popular decadent novels, A Rebours and Là-Bas, were not translated into English until two decades after his death. In America they proved to be thunderbolts; about them storms of controversy broke loose. A Rebours, first translated in 1922, was expurgated. The entire sixth chapter and the episode with the young man at the end of chapter nine were omitted. The passages dealing with Petronius' Satyricon were also bowdlerized.

In 1924, another American publisher became more audacious. Following the French original exactly, with but one or two minor exceptions, he issued Keene Wallis' excellent translation of Là-Bas. Ironically, one critic, writing for the now defunct New York World, mentioned that Là-Bas was not for smut-hunters (1924.9). This chance remark caught the attention of a bluenose. Through his organization for the "suppression of vice" he placed pressure on the publisher. Fearful of costly litigation and bad publicity, the publisher withdrew the novel and even surrendered the plates to the chief smut-hunter.

Introduction

American critics had approved of Là-Bas as a fascinating piece
of literature. They did not dwell on those aspects of the novel that
might prove offensive to some readers. But self-appointed censors
had decided that Là-Bas was a book to be kept from all readers, and
they won out for several years. Because of censorship, the book became notorious. Soon it was "pushed" exclusively by book dealers
who stacked Lady Chatterley's Lover, Ulysses, and Là-Bas side by
side (1962.3).

When Down Stream (A Vau-l'Eau) appeared in 1927, it met with no
opposition. Bluenoses were sniffing elsewhere, but there was little
in the volume to arouse their ire; and despite the lack of notoriety
bestowed upon Là-Bas and A Rebours, Down Stream sold. Delightfully
designed for American readers, the volume gave evidence of a Huysmans'
cult in the United States. These Huysmansians, as they dubbed themselves, could now read from one volume translations of A Vau-l'Eau,
Marthe, Le Drageoir à épices, and selected essays from Certains and
L'Art moderne.

Down Stream was largely the effort of Samuel Putnam, one of America's outstanding translators. Probably the best translation of
Huysmans' vigorous style, Putnam's volume helped to establish Huysmans in American literary circles and also helped to inaugurate Putnam's reputation as a translator. In England, Huysmans' best translator had been Kegan Paul. His translation of En Route is excellent,
provided his inconsistent bowdlerization is overlooked. Its unex-
pected success as a virtual best-seller in 1896 led him to translate
La Cathédrale; sickness, however, made it necessary for him to turn
the project over to Clara Bell, who turned out a reasonably good
version.

L'Oblat, also rendered into English by Kegan Paul's publishing
house, suffered at the hands of its translator. The translation was
so poor, in fact, that it received unfavorable reviews from those
English-speaking critics unfamiliar with the work in French (1924.8).
One ill-informed reviewer, unaware that L'Oblat was Huysmans' last
novel, complained that Huysmans apparently wrote the work during his
literary novitiate, and that if it had not been written by Huysmans
it would never have been translated (1924.9). L'Oblat has yet to be
rendered into readable English.

Good translations of Huysmans into English have been few, although in academic circles, he has had a good reception. He is read
by students of literature and psychology, by lovers of art and music,
by devotees of decadence and diabolism. The major problem facing
those who read only English is finding Huysmans' books in their own
language. An English translation of his collected works has never
been undertaken, but small publishers have managed to keep his better
known works in print.

Huysmans' strictly naturalistic studies may command little attention; of these, A Vau-l'Eau (1974.14) and En Ménage (1969.20) are the

most readable. When he wrote these short works, the repulsive in
literature was comparatively new, but as a Naturalist Huysmans was
not too widely known even in his own country. Overemphasis on the
loathsome and the morbid cost him readers in his own day; and in our
own his naturalistic novels appear dull for the same reason. Though
they may compare favorably with Zola's novels, they--like most of
Zola's naturalistic studies--are hardly prominent among the best of
world fiction (1974.6).

Lovers of art will always be fascinated by L'Art moderne, Certains, and Trois Eglises et Trois Primitifs (1967.17). Closely
allied with the late nineteenth-century Impressionists, Huysmans
praised their canvases at a time when they were ignored or flouted.
As an art critic, he was the first to announce Degas one of the
world's greatest artists. Pissarro, Manet, and Gauguin were praised
by him long before they attracted the disdain of academic criticism
so prevalent toward the end of the century. To Cézanne, Renoir, and
Rouault, he devoted many words of unqualified praise. From Huysmans
alone descends almost all the valid early criticism of Impressionism.
Significantly, most of his judgments about the Impressionists have
become universally acceptable (1958.6).

Many Huysmansians, though taken up with his art critiques and his
A Rebours or Là-Bas, still regard En Route as Huysmans' best work.
Their opinion received a kind of official confirmation on 26 November 1952. On that date, the front page of the Parisian daily Ce
Matin carried the news that En Route had been selected by a group of
eminent novelists, critics, and scholars as one of the twelve best
French novels of the nineteenth century. Among the jurors who ranked
this minor classic of French literature so highly were such well-known
personalities as André Maurois, François Mauriac, Colette, and
Edouard Herriot. They took into account that Huysmans' novel is a
bit strained, somewhat tedious, and even dated; but in their collec-
tive judgment, En Route still deserved the honor they accorded it.

Never could Huysmans have suspected that he would merit the attention he has received in England and America over almost a full
century. To focus on that attention bibliographically is the chief
objective of this Reference Guide. Part I lists all known translations of Huysmans' works into English. Part II provides annotations
of all major studies in English dealing directly with Huysmans, as
well as peripheral books, articles, and reviews of value. Secondary
references that simply echo other more important sources have been
omitted; only those reviews that have some critical or incidental importance have been considered. Doctoral dissertations and masters
theses that are included have made some contribution to Huysmansian
scholarship.

This Reference Guide would not have been possible, obviously,
without the scholarship and critical attention of all those who, to
one degree or another, have manifested some interest in Huysmans. To
them, I am most indebted. I am also indebted to many others: to the

Introduction

Personnel and Budget Committee of the English Department of St. John's College and the Administration of St. John's University for a reduced teaching schedule during the Fall 1978 semester; to the Reference Librarians at St. John's University Library, especially Anna Donnelly and Julie Cunningham, for their help in running down leads and obtaining innumerable interlibrary loans; to the Reference Librarians at the New York Public Library, where I conducted much of my initial research; to Dr. Marilyn Gaull for her valuable suggestions and editorial assistance; and, finally, to former students in my Aestheticism and Decadence seminars, from whom I learned so much in teaching them about the life, works, career, and influence of Joris-Karl Huysmans.

Part I
The Works of Huysmans
and Their Translations into English

Le Drageoir à épices (1874)

Marthe, histoire d'une fille (1876)

"Camaieu in Red," [excerpt of one prose poem] in Stuart Merrill's Pastels in Prose (New York: Harpers, 1890), pp. 105-107.

"Camaieu in Red," [Stuart Merrill's translation] in Two Worlds Monthly 2 (February 1927), 358.

"Dish of Spices," in Samuel Putnam's Down Stream (Chicago: Covici, 1927), pp. 187-261.

Ibid. (New York: Fertig, 1975).

"Marthe," in Samuel Putnam's Down Stream (Chicago: Covici, 1927), pp. 5-114.

Marthe. Putnam translation; illustrated by Toulouse-Lautrec (New York: Lear, 1948).

"Marthe," [translator not acknowledged] in Four Fallen Women (New York: Dell, 1953), pp. 9-80.

Marthe. Translated by Robert Baldick (London: Fortune Press, 1958).

Works and Translations

"Emile Zola et L'Assommoir"
(1876)

"Emile Zola and L'Assommoir,"
[translator not acknowledged] in
Documents of Modern Literary Realism, edited by George J. Becker
(Princeton Univ. Press, 1963),
pp. 230-35.

Les Soeurs Vatard (1879)

Not translated.

"Sac au dos" (1880)

"Sac au dos." Translated by L. G.
Meyer. In Short Story Classics,
edited by William Patten (New York:
B. F. Collier & Son, 1907),
pp. 1515-55.

"Sac au dos." Translated by L. G.
Meyer. In Great Modern French
Stories, edited by W. H. Wright
(New York: Liveright, 1917),
pp. 268-297.

"Knapsack." Translated by H.
Roche. In Great French Short
Stories, edited by Benjamin and
R. Hargreaves (New York: Boni &
Liveright, 1928), pp. 872-902.

Croquis parisiens (1880)

Parisian Sketches. Translated with
Introduction and Notes by Richard
Griffiths (London: Fortune Press,
1962).

En Ménage (1881)

Living Together. Translated with
Introduction and Notes by J. W. G.
Sandiford-Pellé (London: Fortune
Press, 1969).

Pierrot sceptique [written in
collaboration with Léon Hennique]
(1881)

Not translated.

A Vau-l'Eau (1882)

Down Stream. Translated with a
Preface by Samuel Putnam (Chicago:
Covici, 1927), pp. 115-85.

2

Ibid. (New York: Fertig, 1975).

Downstream. Translated by Robert Baldick (London: Fortune Press, 1952).

"Monsieur Folatin," [translator not acknowledged] in French Stories and Tales, edited by S. Geist (New York: Knopf, 1954), pp. 218–59.

Ibid. (New York: Pocket Library, 1956), pp. 218–59.

L'Art moderne (1883)

"Of Dilettantism," [excerpt of one essay] in Samuel Putnam's Down Stream (Chicago: Covici, 1927), pp. 265–70.

Ibid. (New York: Fertig, 1975).

A Rebours (1884)

Against the Grain. Translated by John Howard; introduction by Havelock Ellis (New York: Lieber & Lewis, 1922).

Ibid. (New York: Boni, 1923).

Ibid. (1926).

Against the Grain: A Novel Without a Plot. Translator not acknowledged. Private, limited edition (Paris: Groaves & Michaux, 1926).

Against the Grain. Translator not acknowledged [John Howard] (Chicago: Argus, c. 1928).

Ibid. (New York: Modern Library, 1930).

Ibid. (Toronto: McLeod, 1930).

Ibid. (New York: Hartsdale House, 1931).

Ibid. (New York: Three Sirens, 1931).

3

Against the Grain. Translator not
acknowledged (London: Fortune
Press, 1931).

Against the Grain. Translator not
acknowledged [John Howard]; introduction by Havelock Ellis (Toronto:
Ambassador, 1946).

Ibid.   (New York: Hartsdale House,
1946).

Against the Grain. Translator not
acknowledged [John Howard] (New
York: Blue Ribbon Books, 1949).

Against the Grain. Translator not
acknowledged (London: Fortune
Press, 1951).

Against the Grain. Translator not
acknowledged [John Howard] (New
York: Random House, 1956).

Against Nature. Translated with an
Introduction by Robert Baldick
(London: Penguin, 1959).

Excerpt from Chapter V [on Gustave
Moreau] in From Classicists to the
Impressionists: Art and Architec-
ture in the Nineteenth Century.
Vol. III of A Documentary History
of Art, edited by Elizabeth Gilmore
Holt (New York: Anchor Books,
Doubleday, 1966), pp. 483-88.
Taken from the Modern Library edi-
tion of 1930; pp. 141-50, 154-56.

Two selections in Aesthetes and
Decadents of the 1890's, edited by
Karl Beckson (New York: Random
House, Vintage Books, 1966).   The
translation is John Howard's.   The
first selection is from Chapter I,
and is found between pages 270-74
of Beckson's anthology; the second
is from Chapter V, between pages
274-80.

	Against the Grain. Translator not acknowledged [John Howard]; introduction by Havelock Ellis (New York: Dover, 1969).

En Rade (1887)   Not translated.

Un Dilemme (1887)   Not translated.

Certains (1889)   Three essays, "Degas," "Felicien Rops," and "Gustave Moreau," in Samuel Putnam's Down Stream (Chicago: Covici, 1927), pp. 276–81, 282–315, 271–75.

Ibid. (New York: Fertig, 1975).

"Cézanne" [translator not acknowledged] in Elizabeth Gilmore Holt's From Classicists to the Impressionists: Art and Architecture in the Nineteenth Century. Vol. III of A Documentary History of Art (New York: Anchor Books, Doubleday, 1966), pp. 488–89.

La Bièvre (1890)   Not translated.

Là-Bas (1891)   Down There. Translated by Keene Wallis (New York: Boni, 1924).

Ibid. (Paris: Privately printed, 1928).

Down There. Translator not acknowledged; introduction by Lucien Descaves (London: Fortune Press, 1930).

Là-Bas. Translated by Keene Wallis (Chicago: Black Archer Press, 1935).

Là-Bas. Translator not acknowledged; edited with notes by Alan H. Walton (London: Fortune Press, 1946).

Là-Bas. Translator not acknowledged (London: Fortune Press,
1950).

Là-Bas. Translator not acknowledged (Paris: Collection Le Ballet
des Muses, c. 1950).

Là-Bas. Translator not acknowl-
edged; edited with notes by
Montague Summers (London: Fortune
Press, 1952).

Down There. Translated by Keene
Wallis (Evanston, Ill.: University
Books, 1956).

Down There. Translated by Keene
Wallis; introduction by Robert
Baldick (Evanston, Ill.: Universi-
ty Books, 1958).

"The Karlsruhe 'Crucifixion.'"
Extract from Chapter I; translated
by Robert Baldick in Grunewald
(London: Phaidon Press, 1958),
pp. 7-9.

Down There. Translator not
acknowledged (New York: Wehman,
1959).

Là-Bas. Translated by Keene
Wallis (New York: Dover, 1972).

Down There. Translator not
acknowledged (London: Sphere
Books, 1974).

En Route (1895)

En Route. Translated with a prefatory note by Kegan Paul (London:
K. Paul, Trench, Truber, 1896).

Ibid., 2nd ed. (1896).

Ibid., 3rd ed. (1908).

Ibid., 4th ed. (1918).

Ibid. (New York: Dutton, 1918).

Ibid. (1920).

"Welding of Souls," [excerpt] in
Catholic World, 162 (November
1945), 172-173.

En Route. Translated with a prefatory note by Kegan Paul (New York:
Fertig, 1976).

La Cathédrale (1898)

The Cathedral. Translated by Clara
Bell; edited with a prefatory note
by Kegan Paul (London: K. Paul,
Trench, Trubner, 1898).

Ibid. (New York: New Amsterdam
Book Company, 1898).

Ibid. (London: K. Paul, Trench,
Trubner, 1922).

Ibid. (1925).

Ibid. (New York: Dutton, 1925).

The Cathedral: Chartres. Abridged
from the Kegan Paul translation and
edited by H. Trudgian (New York:
Nelson, 1936).

La Bièvre et Saint-Séverin
(1898)

Not translated.

La Magie en Poitou: Gilles des
Rais (1899)

Not translated.

La Bièvre; Les Gobelins;
Saint-Séverin (1901)

Not translated.

Sainte Lydwine de Schiedam
(1901)

St. Lydwine of Schiedam. Translated by Agnes Hastings (London:
K. Paul, 1923).

Ibid. (New York: Dutton, 1923).

Works and Translations

De Tout (1902)   Not translated.

Esquisse biographique sur Don   Not translated.
Bosco (1902)

L'Oblat (1903)   The Oblate. Translated by
E. Perceval (London: K. Paul, 1924).

Ibid. (New York: Dutton, 1924).

"Death of a Cat," [excerpt; translated by Eric Posselt] in Golden Book of Cat Stories, edited by Era Zistel (Chicago: Ziff-Davis, 1946), pp. 197-98.

The Oblate. Translated by E. Perceval (New York: Fertig, 1977).

Trois Primitifs (1905)   "The Grunewalds in the Colmar Museum," [slightly shortened chapter translated by Robert Baldick] in Grunewald (London: Phaidon Press, 1958), pp. 10-25.

Le Quartier Notre-Dame (1905)   Not translated.

Les Foules de Lourdes (1906)   Crowds of Lourdes. Translated with a preface by W. H. Mitchell (London: Burns, Oates, 1925).

Ibid. (New York: Benziger, 1925).

Trois Eglises et Trois   Not translated.
Primitifs (1908)

Part II
Writings about Huysmans in English, 1880-1978

1880

1 BOURGET, PAUL. "Paris Letter: July 1880." _Academy_, 18 (31 July), 78-81.
  Review of _Croquis parisiens_. These sketches provide curious pictures of the poor quarters of Paris. The author, an admirer of Dickens, often employs the method of the great novelist to depict the smallest details of miserable subjects. The style is close to that of Baudelaire and the Goncourts; yet the prose is "certainly the most Byzantine product of our epoch."

1883

1 ANON. "French Literature." _Saturday Review_, 56 (7 July), 30.
  Review of _L'Art moderne_. The criticism is "a curious mixture of native shrewdness, ludicrous prejudice, and the misappreciation which the absence of wide and patient reading and cultivation naturally causes." Written by one of M. Zola's "young men," its style may amuse some readers, but it is "entirely beneath criticism."

1884

1 MOORE, GEORGE. "A Curious Book." _St. James Gazette_, 8 (2 September), 6-7.
  Moore called _A Rebours_ "a prodigious book . . . a beautiful mosaic." _Huysmans'_ novel struck him as one of the greatest books in the whole history of literature; yet a work "so exotic it was fit only for the literary gourmet." Furthermore, this "curious book" broke the hold that Zola and the Naturalists had on fiction.

1888

1888

1 MOORE, GEORGE. Confessions of a Young Man. London: Swan,
      Sonnenschein, Lowrey; New York: Bretano's, pp. 217-18.
         "A page of Huysmans is as a dose of opium, a glass of
      something exquisite and spiritous," Moore wrote. "Huysmans
      goes to my soul like a gold ornament of Byzantine workman-
      ship; there is in his style the yearning charm of arches, a
      sense of ritual, the passion of the Gothic. . . ." Like an
      Irish Des Esseintes, Moore confessed he too longed "for ex-
      cess, for crime." Underscoring his Des Esseintes-like na-
      ture, he wrote: "I am feminine, morbid, perverse. But
      above all perverse; almost everything perverse interests,
      fascinates me."
         Reprinted: 1889.1; 1892.1; 1901.8; 1904.3; 1906.2;
      1907.14; 1911.2; 1915.3; 1917.5; 1918.2; 1923.12; 1926.3;
      1928.5; 1929.5; 1933.4; 1937.2; 1939.3; 1943.1; 1952.6;
      1961.6. [Since its initial publication, Moore's Confes-
      sions has had so many editions, revisions, and expansions
      that the reader interested in the details of each is ad-
      vised to consult Edwin Gilcher's A Bibliography of George
      Moore (Dekalb, Ill.: North Illinois Univ. Press, 1970).]

1889

1 MOORE, GEORGE. Confessions of a Young Man. London: Swan,
      Sonnenschein.
         [See note appended to 1888.1.]

1891

1 ANON. "French Literature." Saturday Review, 71 (2 May), 543.
         Review of Là-Bas. The author has executed his purpose--
      to treat of demoniality, Black Masses, Gilles de Rais--
      "with some skill."

2 ANON. "Naturalism v. Decadence." National Observer, 6
      (20 June), 126.
         Review of Zola's L'Argent and Huysmans' Là-Bas. In
      spite of its "brilliance and erudition," Là-Bas is not a
      complete success: "its author is too self-consciously
      decadent to convince." Zola's novel is "tedious reading."

1   MOORE, GEORGE. Confessions of a Young Man. London: Swan,
     Sonnenschein.
         [See note appended to 1888.1.]

2   SYMONS, ARTHUR. "J.-K. Huysmans." Fortnightly Review, 51
     (March), 402-14.
         However Huysmans' novels are regarded, they are "the
     sincere and complete expression of a remarkable personali-
     ty." To realize how faithfully he has revealed himself in
     all he has written, it is necessary to know the man. [A
     bio-psychological analysis follows with comments on Le
     Drageoir à épices, Marthe, En Ménage, Croquis parisiens,
     L'Art moderne, and A Rebours.] As for Huysmans' style,
     "he manipulates the French language with a freedom some-
     times barbarous, 'dragging his images by the heels or the
     hair' (in the admirable phrases of M. Leon Bloy) 'up and
     down the worm-eaten staircases of terrified syntax,' gain-
     ing the effects at which he aims." No one before Huysmans
     had ever so realized the perverse charm of the artificial.
     His psychology is a matter of the sensations, chiefly the
     visual. "To M. Huysmans the world appears to be a pro-
     foundly uncomfortable, unpleasant, ridiculous place, with
     a certain solace in various forms of art. . . ."
         Reprinted in abbreviated form in 1916.2; with additions
     in 1916.3; and in full in 1919.7.

1   ANON. "Notes." Nation, 56 (2 February), 84-85.
         Tells of the recent death of ex-Abbé Boullan, the Doc-
     teur Johannès of Là-Bas. It relates how the Abbé, in his
     earlier years, was director of a convent of nuns whom he
     instructed in mystical theology. Some of the nuns became
     inspired; some apparently bewitched. Boullan was con-
     demned by his archbishop and excommunicated by Rome.
     Thereafter he devoted himself to the occult. Huysmans met
     with him to complete his research for Là-Bas. American
     readers who have taken to "so deliberately repulsive a
     writer as M. Huysmans . . . will hear with a certain inter-
     est of the Abbé's death at Lyons."

2   SYMONS, ARTHUR. "The Decadent Movement in Literature."
     Harper's Magazine, 87 (November), 858-67.
         General discussion of "the latest movement in European
     literature." Alludes to the Goncourts, Verlaine, Mallarmé,
     Maeterlinck, and Huysmans. Huysmans "demands a prominent

1894

place in any record of the Decadent movement," for his work is largely determined by the <u>maladie fin de siècle</u>. Comments on <u>Marthe</u>, <u>Les Soeurs Vatard</u>, <u>En Ménage</u>, <u>Là-Bas</u>, and <u>A Rebours</u>. Huysmans' exceptional achievement is <u>A Rebours</u>: "it is there that he has expressed not merely himself, but an epoch."
    Reprinted: 1918.5.

1894

1   ANON. "A Disciple of Emile Zola." <u>Review of Reviews</u> [New York], 10 (July), 93.
    [Comments on an article written by Jules Moog which had appeared in <u>Nouvelle Revue</u>, May 15, 1894.] Huysmans, who at one time claimed Zola as his master, possesses a complex literary personality. From realism he turned to mysticism. <u>En Ménage</u> is Huysmans' "greatest triumph in the world of fiction; for in it he has given a marvelous picture of a certain section of French society." <u>A Rebours</u> and <u>Là-Bas</u> are also worthy of praise; in writing the latter he had to study the strange subjects with which he deals. His descriptions of "<u>La Messe Noire</u> and other demonological scenes are full of terrible eloquence and weird power."

2   HUNEKER, JAMES GIBBONS. "Huysmans." <u>Musical Courier</u>, 29 (11 July), 9.
    <u>Là-Bas</u> gratifies one's taste for the occult; it is a novel certain "to melt your teeth and grizzle your hair with horror." Huysmans' vivid style, with its enormous vocabulary and complex, carefully varied sentence structure, is used effectively to describe and evoke sensations, particularly unpleasant ones. Huysmans is now the greatest master in French prose "since poor Maupassant went to Hell's Foundry."

1895

1   ANON. "En Route." <u>Guardian</u> [London], 50 (7 August), 1174.
    Review of <u>En Route</u>. The merit of this book lies in the force and simplicity with which it focuses on the realities of religion and the mystic's life detached from the world. Basically, the novel is "the story of a modern man of letters . . . artistic and critical . . . flung upon the full tide of Parisian materialism and sensuality and for twenty years and more swimming with the tide, finding himself when over forty . . . yielding himself with generous candour to conversion and reconciliation."

2   ANON. "M. Huysmans' Conversion." Speaker [London], (18 May),
      pp. 540-41.
         Review of En Route. The novel made Huysmans "the lit-
      erary sensation of the hour in the French capital." Though
      its author has "a capacity for squandering his soul on pa-
      per," his book can be recommended "to the lover of Church
      music and Church ritual, to those interested in the psycho-
      logical process of religious conversion."

3   ANON. "Worship of the Devil in Paris." Literary Digest [New
      York], 11 (3 August), 408.
         Discusses and quotes from an article Huysmans published
      in the 15 June 1895 issue of Le Figaro concerning diaboli-
      cal possession, in which he displayed considerable antago-
      nism to secret societies and devil-worshippers.

4   DERECHEF, RALPH. "French Books." National Observer [Edin-
      burgh], 14 (1 June), 90.
         Review of En Route: "another Pilgrim's Progress."
      Though called tedious by some critics, Huysmans' novel will
      hold the attention of the more serious reader. "The work
      is worthy of the craftsman . . . pages upon pages . . . are
      absolutely flawless."

5   NORDEAU, MAX. Degeneration. [Translated from the second edi-
      tion of the German Work.] New York: Appleton, pp. 298-310.
         Equates decadence with disease. Attacks Huysmans in a
      chapter entitled "Decadents and Aesthetes." As an author,
      Huysmans monstrously exaggerated the faults of Gautier and
      Baudelaire. As a man, he is "the classical type of the
      hysterical mind without originality. . . ." A red thread
      of lubricity runs through all his books. As a languishing
      Decadent, he is "as vulgarly obscene as when he was a
      bestial Naturalist." A Rebours "can scarcely be called a
      novel." Là-Bas is "repulsive" and "silly," a book that
      "furnishes M. Huysmans with the opportunity of burrowing
      and sniffing with swinish satisfaction into the most hor-
      rible filth."

6   [SYMONS, ARTHUR]. "M. Huysmans as a Mystic." Saturday Re-
      view, 79 (9 March), 312-13.
         Traces Huysmans' literary and spiritual evolution from
      his days as a Naturalist to his writing of En Route. Few
      cases could be of greater interest to the student of psy-
      chology than the development of Huysmans' mind. His life
      can be summed up as "an ascending spiral, an enigmatical
      but always ascending spiral of the soul."
         Reprinted: 1897.6.

1896

1896

1　ANON. "A Fastidious Convert." <u>Literary World</u> [London], 54
　　　(25 September), 227-28.
　　　　Review of Kegan Paul's translation of <u>En Route</u>: "a re-
　　　markable book, a stirring book, a kind of <u>Robert Elsmer</u> for
　　　Roman Catholics." The translation is excellent and the
　　　translator's preface helps us understand the writer. De-
　　　spite its weak plot, the novel can be recommended to anyone
　　　with a taste for theological problems. The only disappoint-
　　　ing thing about the book is that it ends "without any par-
　　　ticular result."

2　ANON. "A <u>fin-de-siècle</u> Pilgrim's Progress." <u>Review of Re-
　　　views</u> [London], 14 (August), 173-84.
　　　　Detailed discussion of Kegan Paul's translation of <u>En
　　　Route</u> with a summary and lengthy quotations from the novel.
　　　A "<u>Pilgrim's Progress</u> done in the style of the artist," the
　　　novel depicts "the flight of the convicted sinner from the
　　　City of Destruction to Mount Zion, in the very latest dia-
　　　lect of modernity."

3　ANON. "En Route." <u>Critic</u>, 29 (5 December), 358-59, 364.
　　　　Review of Kegan Paul's translation of <u>En Route</u>. The
　　　main character, Durtal, "takes a strong hold upon the read-
　　　er." The translation is excellent, and the overall quality
　　　of the book prevents it from being dull, even to those who
　　　may have little interest in the subject matter.

4　ANON. "Reviews." <u>Humanitarian</u>, 9 (December), 465-70.
　　　　Review of Kegan Paul's translation of <u>En Route</u>: "the
　　　translation may be considered one of the most perfect ren-
　　　derings of any French author that has yet seen the light
　　　of England." The novel is an interesting psychological
　　　study that contains "mysticism common to all creeds, and
　　　indeed to all humanity, and much of that struggle between
　　　the lower and higher nature which every man experiences
　　　sooner or later."

5　ANON. "Whither?" <u>Saturday Review</u>, 82 (8 August), 139.
　　　　Review of Kegan Paul's translation of <u>En Route</u>: "a re-
　　　markably dull book." The quality of the translation "en-
　　　hances the volume's unreadableness."

6　GRAY, JOHN. "The Redemption of Durtal." <u>Dial</u>, no. 4,
　　　pp. 7-11.
　　　　Essay on <u>Là-Bas</u> and <u>En Route</u>. Focuses on Durtal's re-
　　　pentance, "the penitent being a man of profound baseness"

with his spiritual progress narrated "as far as an author dare, and as exhaustively as skill and patience are capable." Waxes enthusiastically about Huysmans' "control"; gives examples of his "dexterity." Ends with the comment that even "at the point of utmost progress in En Route, Durtal was still at the beginning of the purgative life."

7   GULL, RANGER. "En Route." Academy, 50 (28 October), 304-305.
        Review of Kegan Paul's translation of En Route: "a rare work, and not to be carelessly read." It is not difficult to understand why this novel has been received with enthusiasm both here and on the continent. Unfortunately, from an ethical point of view, the book promotes egocentricity and fails to deal with "duty." As literature, however, the novel deserves "unsparing praise"; so, too, Kegan Paul for his "spirited English version."

8   [HAKE, ALFRED E.] Regeneration, A Reply to Max Nordeau. New York: Putnam's Sons, p. 273.
        Refutation of Nordeau's Degeneration (see 1895.5) as the work of a "scientifically superstitious man who distorts reality." Brief discussion of A Rebours and its hero, Des Esseintes. "We are fully convinced that Nordeau is no Duc Des Esseintes at heart, masquerading as a benefactor of humanity. . . ."

9   LE GALLIENNE, RICHARD. "New Books." Statist (20 June), p. 903.
        Review of Kegan Paul's translation of En Route. "The literary power of this book is amazing." Unique as a picture of monastic life, there is yet "a sickliness of taste about it, an unpleasant unctuousness." The spirituality is mainly "perverted sensuality."

10   PAUL, KEGAN. "Translator's Note," in his translation of En Route. 1st and 2nd eds. London: K. Paul, Trench, Trubner, pp. v-xi.
        States that he has tried to make his translation "as full and as faithful" as possible. Notes that the work was written for a Catholic audience in France, however, not a Protestant one in England; that the two nations have different ways of viewing Christianity and human nature; that he has "softened" certain of Huysmans' "blunt passages out of regard for English modesty." Briefly explains how Huysmans came to write the novel and that it would be "intrusive and impertinent" to identify the author too closely with Durtal, the protagonist. Finally, he

1896

> hopes that the novel "may speak to the hearts of many men
> in England as it seems to have already done in France."
> Reprinted: 1908.1; 1918.3; 1920.3; 1976.15.

11   PECK, HARRY THURSTON. "A Novel of Mysticism." Bookman [New
      York], 4 (November), 240-45.
        Discussion of En Route, "which one may without exaggera-
tion think not only the greatest novel of the day, but one
of the most important, because it is one of the most char-
acteristic books of our quarter of the century." Unique in
style and spirit among Huysmans' books, this spiritual
autobiography is an odd mixture of medievalism and modernity.
      Reprinted: 1898.17.

1897

1   ANON. "En Route." Catholic World, 64 (January), 543-44.
        Review of En Route: "a remarkable piece of testimony to
the power of the spirit over the flesh." The quasi-personal
character of the disclosures of Durtal-Huysmans is based
upon precedents afforded in the works of George Sand,
George Eliot, Lord Byron and others who wrote in front of
a mental mirror reflecting their own inmost thoughts.

2   ANON. "Recent Books--French and English." Blackwood's Maga-
      zine, 161 (April), 455-62.
        Review of En Route: "on the whole . . . very remarkable
and well worthy of consideration." Relates the narrative
and supplies several long quotations to indicate Huysmans'
style. That a sordid realist like Huysmans could produce
this "Pilgrim's Progress" is extraordinary.

3   ANON. "Recent Fiction." Nation, 65 (1 July), 18.
        Review of Kegan Paul's translation of En Route. The
traditions of the Church--its music, architecture, ritual,
and imposing functions--are freely used to obtain effects
"sometimes intensely dramatic and sometimes cheaply theat-
rical." The book, however, has been written "with notice-
able literary force and skill."

4   HENRY, STUART. "M. Huysmans," in his Hours With Famous
      Parisians. Chicago: Way & Williams, pp. 113-18.
        Describes Huysmans as serious, quizzical, reverential,
Bohemian, "a quiet little man with small pointed mustache
and beard neatly clipped." He has "a rather bright eye and
a squirrel look." Speaking in a low tone, without gestures
or flourishes, he mixes religion, mysticism, hope, despair

and indifference in his conversation. To document a novel, he explains, takes two years: "two years of hard work. That is the trouble with the naturalistic novel--it requires so much documentary care." His next book, he adds, will be on the Cathedral at Chartres. "The relations of the little grocery girl with the proprietor of the wine shop on the corner have been thoroughly exploited. Nothing remains untouched but Catholicism and its art."

5 MOURNEY, GABRIEL. "Joris Karl Huysmans." Fortnightly Review, 67 (1 March), 409-23.
   Huysmans' early works are discussed; A Rebours dwelt upon at length; analyses of En Route and La Cathédrale follow. Agitation, ambition, and worldly care touch him no more. The drama which runs through Huysmans' whole work is "the evolution of a soul."

6 SYMONS, ARTHUR. "M. Huysmans as a Mystic," in his Studies in Two Literatures. London: Leonard Smithers, pp. 299-305.
   Reprint of 1895.6. [This chapter together with the chapter "Huysmans as a Symbolist" in the first edition of The Symbolist Movement (see 1899.6) were merged into a single essay, "The Later Huysmans," which appeared in the second edition of The Symbolist Movement (1908.2), and in volume 8 of Symons' Collected Works (1924.10).]

1898

1 ANON. "Academy Portraits: J.-K. Huysmans." Academy, 55 (22 October), 126-27.
   Describes Huysmans' Parisian apartment, "from which one might almost be said to be able to read [his] life history." Things worldly and things spiritual mark the two extremes of his life. Discusses his library and his works. Refers to the autobiographical nature of his fiction and the methods of his literary composition--extensive research, voluminous note taking, and the mastering of his subject before the more creative part of his writing takes place.

2 ANON. "Belles Lettres." Westminster Review, 149 (June), 712-13.
   Review of Clara Bell's translation of La Cathédrale. Through the style is "admirable," the novel lacks "human interest." The mental and spiritual development of the main character does not absorb the attention sufficiently to allow full enjoyment of "this recrudescence of medieval

1898

> mysticism." The translation is "readable and intelligent," but fails to convey Huysmans' strongest literary characteristics.

3   ANON. "Books of the Week." Guardian, no. 16, 115 (5 April), p. 5.
> Review of Clara Bell's translation of La Cathédrale: "an unusually intelligent translation which preserves . . . the colour and spirit of the original." The reader who cannot appreciate the encyclopedic learning of this book will nonetheless find "many magnificent pages to admire, especially the description of Chartres Cathedral." Though decidedly inferior to En Route, which is "M. Huysmans' masterpiece," this unique volume is still "a fine addition to French literature."

4   ANON. "Decadent, Mystic, Catholic." Academy, 53 (19 February), 196-97.
> Review of La Cathédrale. On the whole, the novel is disappointing, though parts may be excellent. "M. Huysmans' picture of the Cathedral stands out with the force and delicacy of a nocturne by his friend Mr. Whistler."

5   ANON. "Fiction." Literature [London], no. 26 (26 March), pp. 353-54.
> Review of Clara Bell's translation of La Cathédrale. This translation of a very difficult book is "remarkably satisfactory"; eliminated are many of Huysmans' "strange technical expressions and antiquated diction." Though devoid of incident and movement and opposed to all laws of fiction, this novel is "one of the most remarkable books in contemporary literature."

6   ANON. "Fiction." Scotsman, no. 17,081 (24 March), p. 9.
> Review of Clara Bell's translation of La Cathédrale. Those who can read this book in the spirit in which it was written will find "it shares all the charms of the author's previous works." To the merely curious it may be of interest as "a study in medievalism . . . a cast of thought that is strangely foreign to that of the common man."

7   ANON. "Huysmans' Cathedral." Glascow Herald, 93 (24 March), 7.
> Review of La Cathédrale: "will stand as a very remarkable monument of a literary conversion wrought, not . . . by sorrow and misfortune, but by the influence of art."

8   ANON. "Mystic Fiction." Commercial Advertiser [New York],
      (30 April), p. 10.
         Review of Clara Bell's translation of La Cathédrale.
      This is "a curious combination of a Baedeker guide book,
      a Life of the Saints, and a black-letter volume of "mysti-
      cal rhapsodies." Although not really a novel and "quite
      unreadable," the interest of this work lies in learning
      something about the intellectual and ethical life of France
      today.

9   ANON. "Recent Novels." Times [London], no. 35, 573
      (20 July), p. 15.
         Review of Clara Bell's translation of La Cathédrale.
      The work can hardly be classified as a novel; it has no
      plot and little in the way of characterization. What it is
      can only be called "a work of a writer of marked individu-
      ality, with a talent for psychological analysis."

10   ANON. "Romans and Anglican." Spectator, 80 (26 March),
      439-40.
         Review of Clara Bell's translation of La Cathédrale.
      This is "a curious if not very edifying work . . . a hodge-
      podge of stale medievalism . . . childish and fantastic
      imaginings." Roman and Protestant theology have many ex-
      amples of nobler mysticism than that exhibited in this
      novel.

11   ANON. "The Cathedral." Literary World [London], 57
      (15 April), 342-43.
         Review of Clara Bell's translation of La Cathédrale.
      This work is more than an elaborate guide to Chartres: it
      further expands the spiritual struggles of the protagonist
      of En Route. Despite a few slips, this translation is
      "very readable."

12   ANON. "The Cathedral." Review of Reviews, 17 (15 April),
      399.
         Review of Clara Bell's translation of La Cathédrale:
      "an attempt to familiarise us with the symbolism of the
      Middle Ages." The cathedral is Chartres and readers will
      find the book "a valuable guide."

13   ANON. "The Conversion of a Realist." Outlook [London], 1
      (12 February), 50-51.
         Review of La Cathédrale. There is no story, and very
      little character. "The book is frigid where it should be
      full of warmth and colour; it is so crammed with facts,
      that it more nearly resembles a guide-book than a hymn of
      praise."

14   COURTNEY, W. L. "Books of the Day." <u>Daily Telegraph</u> [London], no. 13,369 (16 March), p. 6.
        Three novels will always be associated with the strange history of Huysmans: <u>Là-Bas</u>, a "hideous book . . . composed on a repulsive theme"; <u>En Route</u>, "one of the most striking pictures ever penned of the struggles of a vacillating and self-tormenting soul"; and <u>La Cathédrale</u>, "a wonderful picture . . . of the inner meaning of Gothic architecture."
        Reprinted: 1904.1.

15   ELLIS, HAVELOCK. "Huysmans," in his <u>Affirmations</u>. London: Walter Scott, pp. 158–211.
        Four-part essay that attempts "to represent the man who wrote the extraordinary books grouped around <u>A Rebours</u> and <u>En Route</u>." Part I considers "race and environment"; but there is no way to account for Huysmans' genius other than to note that "his sensitive nervous system and extravagant imagination were under the control of a sane and forceful intellect." His sole preoccupation was with his own impressions. He fell under the influence of Baudelaire; then the Goncourts and Zola. The best of his early novels is <u>En Ménage</u>. With <u>A Rebours</u> he attained "to full expression"; perhaps this novel is not his greatest achievement, but it is "the central work in which he has most powerfully concentrated his vision of life." Part II is a discussion of Decadence, Huysmans' concepts of art and predilections in literature. Part III focuses first on <u>L'Art moderne</u> and <u>Certains</u>; concludes that Huysmans' art critiques manifest more than his critical insights: they reveal his own personal vision of the world. A contrast between Huysmans and Zola is drawn. Then discussion of Huysmans' trilogy <u>En Route</u>, <u>La Cathédrale</u>, and <u>L'Oblat</u> follows; these works prove that he is "the greatest master of style, and within his own limits the subtlest thinker and acutest psychologist who . . . uses the medium of the novel." Essentially, Huysmans is less a novelist than a poet with an instinct to use not verse but prose as his medium. Part IV concludes with comments on aspects of beauty, "the whole spiritual cosmogony," and Huysmans as a genius of art.
        Reprinted: 1915.2; 1916.1; 1922.2; 1924.2; 1926.1; 1929.1; 1970.6.
        Reprinted in <u>The New Spirit</u>: 1921.3; 1930.2; 1935.3; 1969.8.
        Reprinted as the Introduction to John Howard's translation of <u>A Rebours</u>: 1931.2; 1946.3; 1969.9. Also in abbreviated form in 1922.3; 1923.7; 1924.3; 1926.2; 1930.3.

16   PAUL, KEGAN. Prefatory note to Clara Bell's translation of
     <u>La Cathédrale</u>. London: K. Paul, Trench, Trubner,
     pp. vii-xi.
          Notes that at the conclusion of <u>En Route</u>, its protago-
     nist stood at the parting of the ways. This sequel indi-
     cates that he has not drifted back into the mire but has
     continued with his pursuit of virtue. Comments in general
     upon Chartres and explains why Huysmans chose this cathe-
     dral for the locale of his novel. As for the narrative,
     there are but four principal characters who exchange views.
     The book resolves itself into a series of dissertations on
     "the Bestiary of Holy Scripture, on church paintings, on
     early pictures, on the mystical and suffering saints of the
     Middle Ages, and on such parts of the flora and fauna as
     have shown themselves most adapted to church decoration."
          Reprinted: 1922.7; 1925.5.

17   PECK, HARRY THURSTON. "Evolution of a Mystic [Huysmans]," in
     his <u>The Personal Equation</u>. New York and London: Harper,
     pp. 135-53.
          Reprint of 1896.11.

18   SYMONS, ARTHUR. "Monsieur Huysmans' New Novel." <u>Saturday Re-</u>
     <u>view</u>, 85 (12 February), 199-200.
          Review of <u>La Cathédrale</u>. The greater part of the book
     is taken up with a study of Chartres and "its elaborate
     and profound symbolism by which 'the soul of sanctuaries'
     slowly reveals itself."
          Reprinted with additions: 1899.6.

19   W., J. E. H. "Paris-Metz-Chartres: A Trilogy of Transla-
     tions." <u>Bookman</u>, 14 (April), 18-19.
          Review of three books, one of which is Clara Bell's
     translation of <u>La Cathédrale</u>: "the most astonishing piece
     of fiction which has been produced in several years." Be-
     cause it lacks a plot and mainly catalogues things mystical
     and symbolical, it makes for "tedious reading." Despite
     Huysmans' "stilted and exaggerated style," Mrs. Bell has
     produced an excellent translation.

<u>1899</u>

1   ANON. "A Tributary of the Seine." <u>Nation</u>, 68 (2 February),
     86-87.
          Comments on <u>La Bièvre et Saint-Séverin</u>: "a picturesque
     guide to the valley of the Bièvre." This book is an in-
     teresting treatment of the ancient streets, quarters, and
     monuments of medieval Paris, where St.-Séverin, an old

church, marks the place where the Bièvre, a small affluent
of the Seine, joins the great river. Though written in
Huysmans' "strange style," this book is worthy to be added
to any collection of works on medieval Paris.

2   ANON. "Modern Mysticism." Quarterly Review, 190 (July-
      October), 79-102.
         Review of nine books, one of which is La Cathédrale:
      "nominally a novel, but in reality a treatise on mystic
      symbolism." The chief value of this work is that it gives
      "a tolerably distinct outline of the type of mystic evolved
      by a modern environment."

3   ANON. "New French Books." Spectator, 82 (14 January), 59-60.
         Review of five books, one of which is La Bièvre et
      Saint-Séverin. In this work, Huysmans has employed his
      double gift of vision and word painting to write about two
      forgotten quarters of Paris. "Those who still haunt the
      Quartier Saint-Séverin, or wander by the bank of the melan-
      choly Bièvre . . . will understand their truth and vivid-
      ness."

4   CRAWFORD, VIRGINIA. "J.-K. Huysmans," in her Studies in For-
      eign Literature. London: Duckworth, pp. 78-105.
         No writer can equal Huysmans in sheer descriptive power.
      This is especially obvious in En Route, "perhaps the most
      extraordinary book of recent years," and in La Cathédrale,
      which is filled with "beautiful writing, of wonderful de-
      scriptive pages, of delicate appreciation, of spiritual in-
      sight into Christian symbolism."
         Reprinted in part in 1900.1 and 1901.6; in full, 1970.5.

5   DOUMIC, RENÉ. "M. J.-K. Huysmans," in his Contemporary French
      Novelists. Translated by Mary D. Frost. New York:
      Crowell, pp. 351-402.
         Discussion of Huysmans' literary endeavors, especially
      En Route--"a very curious and very remarkable book . . . a
      work of edification," with "great" artistic value. En
      Route promises a revival of a new literature, now that
      "Naturalism has perished by its own excesses and positivism
      has seen its best days."

6   SYMONS, ARTHUR. "Huysmans as a Symbolist," in his The Sym-
      bolist Movement in Literature. London: Heinemann,
      pp. 141-50.
         Reprint of 1895.6 combined with 1898.18, plus additions
      and changes.
         Reprinted in revised form: 1908.2; 1919.7.
         Reprinted in part: 1958.9.

7   TAYLOR, H. "Some Aspects of Modern Art." Edinburgh Review,
        190 (July), 48-70.
            Review of six art books, one of which is L'Art moderne
        [60-64]. "The gift of description has been liberally be-
        stowed on M. Huysmans." In writing about Degas, Raffaëlli,
        and Forain, he has established the principles of "the most
        impeccable originators or disciples of the new art."

1900

1   CRAWFORD, VIRGINIA. "Joris-Karl Huysmans." Current Litera-
        ture, 29 (September), 270-71.
            Reprint of a selection abstracted from 1899.4.

1901

1   ANON. "Gossip of French Capital." Chicago Tribune, 60
        (18 August), 6.
            Relates that the anti-clerical laws affect "one of the
        most picturesque figures in the literary world of France--
        namely: J.-K. Huysmans." Notes that, three years before,
        he astonished Paris by giving up his home and Parisian
        friends to reside in the shadow of a monastery at Ligné
        [Liguge]. His house and the abbey had become "a Mecca for
        writers and artists." Now the question is: "What will be-
        come of Huysmans?"

2   ANON. "History and Biography." Westminster Review, 152
        (August), 79-83.
            Review of Sainte Lydwine de Schiedam. Despite Huysmans'
        "grotesque medievalism . . . his style is just as admirable
        as ever." Instead of producing a study of medieval his-
        tory, he has written legendary biography. His medievalism
        triumphs over reason, culture, and refined good sense.

3   ANON. "Literary Notes." Pall Mall Gazette, 72 (15 June), 4.
            Review of Sainte Lydwine de Schiedam. "Except for its
        distinction of style, it does not differ much from lives of
        saints and beatae that one meets with on the shelves of
        Catholic libraries."

4   ANON. "Mystic and Miracle." Academy, 60 (22 June), 527-28.
            Review of Sainte Lydwine de Schiedam. Recounts the ba-
        sic facts of the Saint's life and discusses briefly Huys-
        mans' concept of "mystic substitution." This work of
        sincere though puzzling hagiography is "less interesting
        as literature than as a document."

1901

5   ANON. "Notes of the Day." <u>Literature</u>, 9 (21 September), 266.
        The monks at Ligugé with whom Huysmans has been living
     are being driven from France because of the Associations
     Act. Huysmans will return to Paris.

6   CRAWFORD, VIRGINIA. "Huysmans the Symbolist." <u>Current Liter-
     ature</u>, 30 (May), 586-92.
        Reprint of selection abstracted from 1899.4.

7   HOLLAND, B. "Rome and the Novelists." <u>Edinburgh Review</u>, 194
     (October), 276-301.
        Discussion of eight novels, one of which is <u>En Route</u>:
     "a painfully pathological novel" which describes "the be-
     ginnings of the slow and difficult cleansing in an austere
     Catholic monastery of an imagination stained with the al-
     most indelible hauntings left by a profligate life."

8   MOORE, GEORGE. <u>Confessions of a Young Man</u>. New York:
     Brentano's.
        [<u>See</u> note appended to 1881.1.]

9   MOURNEY, GABRIEL. "The Works of Jean-François Raffaelli."
     <u>International Studio</u>, 14 (July), 3-14.
        Not only was Raffaëlli an excellent painter, but he was
     an excellent etcher too, "as we may discover in the keen
     and characteristic plates illustrating J.-K. Huysmans'
     'Croquis Parisiens.'"

1902

1   ANON. "Literature." <u>Athenaeum</u>, 120 (16 August), 215.
        Review of <u>De Tout</u>. Huysmans' novels have made it obvi-
     ous that he is "one of the great descriptive writers of our
     time, as well as one of the most interesting and unattrac-
     tive individuals." In this book of "scraps and jottings,"
     we have glimpses "of almost every side of his singular
     genius, including some which he has chosen to hide from
     us."

2   ANON. "The Huysmans' Organ." <u>Musical Courier</u>, 45 (20 August),
     14.
        Refers to Des Esseintes' "mouth organ" and alludes to
     Max Nordeau's attack upon Huysmans (<u>see</u> 1895.5). Although
     <u>A Rebours</u> is judged "a powerful and morbid book," it is de-
     scribed [erroneously] as being mainly satire.

3   [BENNETT, ARNOLD]. "A Psychological Enigma." <u>Academy and Literature</u>, 63 (13 September), 251-52.
     Review of <u>De Tout</u>. Huysmans, "one of the most distinguished and adept living artificers of words," can make the reader see what he sees; yet the most interesting thing about Huysmans is the man himself, not his work. This latest book increases the difficulties of comprehending what he is about. These twenty-four miscellaneous essays make up a book that is "simply beautiful from beginning to end."

1903

1   ANON. "Literary Notes." <u>Pall Mall Gazette</u>, 76 (14 March), 1.
     Review of <u>L'Oblat</u>: "contains many lifelike and graceful pictures of monastic life. . . ." Nothing that Huysmans writes is without value, but the text does become "tedious."

2   FERRIS, KATHERINE. "The New Huysmans." <u>Critic</u>, 43 (25 November), 417-22.
     Contrasts the profane Huysmans with the religious. Covers the autobiographical nature of his fiction: "M. Huysmans lurks ill-disguised behind the personality of his principal characters." Focuses on his writing style. Discusses the books written by the "new" Huysmans, <u>En Route</u>, <u>La Cathédrale</u>, and <u>L'Oblat</u>.

3   HUNEKER, JAMES G. "Music and Drama in London." New York <u>Sun</u>, 70 (12 July), Sec. 3, p. 4.
     After discussing music at the Convent Garden, an incidental note refers to Huysmans as "a major force in French letters." Remarks that <u>L'Oblat</u> has not caught the public attention as did <u>En Route</u>, but that its author cares as little for success as failure. Concludes that Huysmans has the ability to make religious functions more entertaining than the dreary erotics of other Parisian writers.

4   L., H. "Paris Letter." <u>Academy and Literature</u>, 64 (18 April), 392-93.
     Discussion of <u>L'Oblat</u>. "Even if it were not a fine piece of literature, it would still be a remarkable and instructive book." Some descriptive passages are "first-rate." As a novel, however, "it is often monstrously heavy and dull."

1904

1904

1   COURTNEY, W. L. "Huysmans: The Cathedral," in his The Devel-
    opment of Maurice Maeterlinck and Other Sketches of Foreign
    Writers. London: G. Richards, pp. 76-84.
        Reprint of 1898.14.

2   HUNEKER, JAMES G. Overtones: A Book of Temperaments. New
    York: Scribner, pp. 204-10.
        Considers the influence of Huysmans on Moore's Evelyn
    Innes: "Joris-Karl Huysmans, that unique disciple of Bau-
    delaire, went to La Trappe and studied religion. George
    Moore, that most plastic-souled Irishman, stayed at home
    and studied Huysmans."
        Reprinted: 1906.1; 1909.3; 1910.2; 1912.1; 1922.5;
    1928.2; 1970.9.

3   MOORE, GEORGE. Confessions of a Young Man. 3rd ed. revised.
    New York: Mitchell Kennerley; London: T. Werner Laurie.
        [See note appended to 1888.1.]

4   SYMONS, ARTHUR. "The Choice," in his Studies in Prose and
    Verse. New York: E. P. Dutton; London: J. M. Dent,
    pp. 101-20.
        Deals with Huysmans' conversion and with A Rebours. Art
    was not finally satisfying without some further reference
    against the world, and so he accepted the Church. Huysmans
    came to realize that "the great choice, the choice between
    the world and something which is not visible in the world
    . . . does not lie in the mere contrast of the subtler and
    the grosser senses. He has come to realize what the choice
    really is, and he has chosen."

5   VIZETELLY, ERNEST ALFRED. Emile Zola: Novelist and Reformer.
    London and New York: J. Lane, pp. 146, 162-63, 191, 207,
    377.
        As a young novelist, Huysmans often "talked literature"
    with Zola, absorbing what he could from "the Master of
    Medan." At times, Huysmans even did research for Zola and
    supplied him with notes that Zola used in documenting his
    fiction.
        Reprinted: 1971.20.

1906

1   HUNEKER, JAMES G. Overtones: A Book of Temperaments. New
    York: Scribner, pp. 204-10.
        Reprint of 1904.2.

2 MOORE, GEORGE. Confessions of a Young Man. New York: Brentano's.
   [See note appended to 1888.1.]

1907

1 ANON. "A Decadent Who Became a Mystic." Current Literature, 43 (July), 54-55.
   Obituary article. Huysmans abandoned the life of the boulevards for the quiet of a Trappist monastery. As a writer, he turned his attention "from decadent psychology to the analysis of religious emotions." Des Esseintes, the symbol of Huysmans' own soul, embodied "the sadness of Ecclesiasticus, the weariness of the Roman aristocracy of the Lower Empire."

2 ANON. "A Significant Novelist." Outlook [New York], 86 (25 May), 134-35.
   Obituary article. Huysmans' books will be eagerly read by those who desire to understand the intellectual and spiritual in processes of the last quarter of the nineteenth century in Europe.

3 ANON. "Huysmans." New York Sun, 74 (14 May), 8.
   Obituary article. Huysmans had it in him to become one of the great names in French literature. If he had kept closer to accepted literary forms he might have become a widely read novelist, but he is likely to remain "an author's author."

4 ANON. "J.-K. Huysmans." Athenaeum, 129 (18 May), 604.
   Obituary article. As a Naturalist, Huysmans saw life "with all the brilliant minuteness of the miniaturist," and was in "the front rank of the school." The greatest of his earliest successes was A Rebours. With Là-Bas he achieved his greatest fame as a novelist. His spiritual evolution is found in En Route, La Cathédrale, and L'Oblat.

5 ANON. "J.-K. Huysmans." Nation and Athenaeum, 1 (18 May), 440.
   Obituary article. Though Huysmans' books lack spontaneity and serenity, they appeal forcibly to a small group of readers. The chief value of his novel A Rebours lies in "its analysis of the over-subtle and morbid emotions of a mind keenly sensitive to artistic impressions."

1907

6 ANON. "Joris-Karl Huysmans." <u>Times Literary Supplement</u>, no. 279 (17 May), pp. 156-57.
   Obituary article. Huysmans, who died on May 12, was one of the last of the Naturalists. With Zola, Daudet, and the Goncourts, he attempted to enlarge the scope of the novel.

7 ANON. "Portraits and World's News." <u>Illustrated London News</u>, 130 (18 May), 750.
   Obituary article. Notes Huysmans joined the Naturalist School and produced some remarkable novels; that from Naturalism he passed to Mysticism; and that he had "a large following and many admirers."

8 ANON. "The Hero With the Artistic Temperament." New York <u>Evening Post</u>, 106 (16 May), 6.
   Obituary article. Notes Huysmans' membership in the Goncourt Academy. Focuses on his work as a Naturalist. As for his books, they are "quite as gross as popular Anglo-Saxon opinion takes contemporary French fiction to be."

9 ANON. "The Literary Week." <u>Academy</u>, 72 (18 May), 475.
   Obituary article. "No more painstaking and conscientious artist than Huysmans ever lived."

10 COMPTON, C. G. "Novelist and Mystic." <u>Outlook</u> [London], 19 (18 May), 657-58.
   Obituary article. Though his life was uneventful, as a writer Huysmans possessed "a rare and peculiar genius." Readers will always find their way to his novels because "he understood the refinement of the senses to its uttermost point, which is reached in mysticism."

11 CONNOLLY, P. J. "The Trilogy of Joris-Karl Huysmans." <u>Dublin Review</u>, 141 (October), 255-71.
   Huysmans' trilogy [<u>En Route</u>, <u>La Cathédrale</u>, <u>L'Oblat</u>] is not wanting in character of thought. Some passages and chapters are unsurpassed for vividness of conception and precision of detail, but the novels "are not sufficiently concatenated by an internal law of development." A strange and complex genius, Huysmans was "a great master of colour and a subtle painter in words."

12 CRAWFORD, VIRGINIA. "Joris-Karl Huysmans." <u>Catholic World</u>, 86 (November), 177-88.
   Huysmans identified the best of Christianity with the monastic life. It is not an exaggeration to assert that without La Trappe his conversion may never have taken hold. Critics who doubted the sincerity of his conversion must

have been silenced by the patience and courage with which
he bore the physical sufferings of the cancer of the mouth
and jaw which finally claimed his life.

13   HUNEKER, JAMES G. "Pessimist's Progress." North American
      Review, 186 (September), 41-54.
            No matter what other qualities persist in Huysmans'
      work, pessimism is never absent. He had a contempt for
      existence, for mediocrity. In incomparable and enamelled
      prose he described the crass ugliness of life. His theme,
      played with variations, was always one of "strangling
      Ennui."
            Reprinted: 1909.4; 1910.3; 1913.1; 1921.5; 1924.5;
      1929.3; 1932.2; 1975.6.

14   MOORE, GEORGE. Confessions of a Young Man. New York:
      Brentano's.
            [See note appended to 1888.1.]

15   PECK, HARRY THURSTON. "One of Three." Bookman [New York],
      25 (July), 462-67.
            Huysmans is one of three writers willing "to lay bare to
      the world their moral and spiritual nakedness." [The other
      two are Bunyan and Rousseau.] From his books can be read a
      genuine spiritual evolution.

16   THOROLD, ALGAR. "Joris-Karl Huysmans." Albany Review, n.s.1
      (September), 680-89.
            Covers the relationship between Huysmans' life and his
      fiction. Focuses on his interest in art and religion. In-
      quires whether his interest in Catholicism was due "in the
      first instance to the exigencies of his literary develop-
      ment or the necessities of his soul."
            Reprinted: 1909.5.

1908

1   PAUL, KEGAN. "Translator's Note," in his translation of En
      Route. 3rd ed. London: K. Paul, Trench, Trubner,
      pp. v-xi.
            Reprint of 1896.10.

2   SYMONS, ARTHUR. "The Later Huysmans," in his The Symbolist
      Movement in Literature. 2nd ed. London: Archibald Consta-
      ble; New York: E. P. Dutton, pp. 136-52.
            Reprint of portions of 1897.6 with additions from 1899.6.
            Reprinted: 1973.13.

1908

3   TONSON, JACOB [pseudonym of ARNOLD BENNETT]. "Books and Per-
     sons." New Age, 3 (27 June), 173-74.
          Discusses briefly an article, "In Memory of Joris-Karl
     Huysmans," by Myriam Harry that appeared in Revue de Paris
     and a serial about Huysmans written by Henry Céard that ran
     in the Revue Hebdomadaire.

1909

1   ANON. "Some Modern Masters in Disillusionment." Current Lit-
     erature, 47 (August), 161-62.
          A discussion of disillusionment in literature with
     lengthy quotations from Algar Thorold's Six Masters in Dis-
     illusionment (see 1909.5).

2   E.[liot], T. S. "Egoists." Harvard Advocate, 88 (5 October),
     16.
          Review of James G. Huneker's Egoists (see 1909.4).
     Judges Huneker's critique of Huysmans "particularly good."
     Labels Huysmans "the genius of faith."

3   HUNEKER, JAMES G. Overtones: A Book of Temperaments. New
     York: Scribner, pp. 204-10.
          Reprint of 1904.2.

4   HUNEKER, JAMES G. "Pessimist's Progress: J.-K. Huysmans,"
     in his Egoists: A Book of Supermen. New York: Scribner,
     pp. 167-206.
          Reprint of 1907.13.

5   THOROLD, ALGAR. "Joris-Karl Huysmans," in his Six Masters in
     Disillusionment. London: Constable, pp. 80-96.
          Reprint of 1907.16.

1910

1   DELAMARRE, LOUIS N. "Huysmans," in Catholic Encyclopedia.
     Vol. VII. New York: Encyclopedia Press, 591.
          Biographical entry. Huysmans was deeply interested in
     the art of the Middle Ages and displayed a fondness for
     mysticism. Both before and after his conversion he was a
     realist. All his work consisted mainly in rendering clear-
     ly details that he had seen and noted down.

2   HUNEKER, JAMES G. Overtones: A Book of Temperaments. New
     York: Scribner, pp. 204-10.
          Reprint of 1904.2.

3   HUNEKER, JAMES G. "Pessimist's Progress: J.-K. Huysmans," in his Egoists: A Book of Supermen. New York: Scribner, pp. 167-206.
      Reprint of 1907.13.

1911

1   CROSNIER, ALEXIS. Latter Day Converts. Translated by Katherine A. Hennessy. Philadelphia: McVey, pp. 13, 40, 44-47, 72-73, 77-79, 89-90, 95, 101, 103.
      Discusses the conversion of five French writers, one of whom is Huysmans, who "took the longest way getting to Rome" after an unhealthy attraction to Satanism.

2   MOORE, GEORGE. Confessions of a Young Man. New York: Brentano's.
      [See note appended to 1888.1.]

1912

1   HUNEKER, JAMES G. Overtones: A Book of Temperaments. New York: Scribner, pp. 204-210.
      Reprint of 1904.2.

2   WRIGHT, C. H. C. A History of French Literature. London: Oxford Univ. Press, pp. 767, 774, 775, 776-77, 801, 803, 859, 883.
      Huysmans was an extraordinary cross between Naturalism and decadent Romanticism. In his books he illustrated "the pathological degeneration of Naturalism beyond the brutality of Zola and the morbidness of the Goncourts." Beginning as a direct follower of Zola, he evolved to A Rebours. He then went from "aesthetic mysticism to a sort of Christian mysticism or Catholic sacerdotalism."
      Reprinted: 1969.24.

1913

1   HUNEKER, JAMES G. "Pessimist's Progress: J.-K. Huysmans," in his Egoists: A Book of Supermen. New York: Scribner, pp. 167-206.
      Reprint of 1907.13.

1913

2   JACKSON, HOLBROOK. The Eighteen Nineties: A Review of Art
       and Ideas at the Close of the Nineteenth Century. London:
       G. Richards; New York: Mitchell Kennerley, pp. 28, 58, 61,
       63, 136, 223.
           The Decadence in England was "an echo of the French
       movement which began with Théophile Gautier, Paul Verlaine
       and Joris-Karl Huysmans." Wilde's Dorian Gray "bears many
       obvious echoes of the most remarkable of French decadent
       novels, the A Rebours of J.-K. Huysmans." Dorian Gray be-
       came the Des Esseintes of English literature; both are
       authentic decadent types. Their differences: "the sensa-
       tions and ideas of Dorian Gray are not elaborated so sci-
       entifically as those of Des Esseintes, but there is some-
       thing more than coincidence in the resemblance of their
       attitudes toward life." Far more than Dorian Gray, A Re-
       bours contains "the apotheosis of the fin de siècle
       spirit."
           Reprinted: 1914.2; 1922.6; 1923.9; 1925.1; 1927.1;
       1931.8; 1934.2; 1939.2; 1950.2; 1966.14; 1976.7.

1914

1   GUILDAY, PETER. "En Route and Church Music." American Cath-
       olic Quarterly, 39 (April), 303-17.
           Durtal, the hero of En Route, liked the Parisian Church
       of St. Sulpice because there he could hear excellent Gre-
       gorian chant. After his conversion he delighted to visit
       other churches to listen to their choirs. Huysmans himself
       found plain song a source of personal inspiration. No one
       has even written so beautifully of the music of the church
       as Huysmans did in En Route.

2   JACKSON, HOLBROOK. The Eighteen Nineties: A Review of Art
       and Ideas at the Close of the Nineteenth Century. New
       York: M. Kennerley, pp. 28, 58, 61, 63, 136, 223.
           Reprint of 1913.2.

1915

1   ALDINGTON, RICHARD. "Decadence and Dynamism." The Egoist, 2
       (1 April), 56-57.
           A Rebours contains "a really marvelous criticism of
       Latin poetry and prose"; but in writing his critiques,
       Huysmans mainly paraphrased and condensed the views of
       Albert Ebert [as expressed in his Allgemeine Geschichte
       der Literatur des Mittelalters].

2   ELLIS, HAVELOCK. "Huysmans," in his <u>Affirmations</u>. Boston:
       Houghton Mifflin, pp. 158-211.
          Reprint of 1898.15.

3   MOORE, GEORGE. <u>Confessions of a Young Man</u>. New York: Modern
       Library.
          [<u>See</u> note appended to 1888.1.]

1916

1   ELLIS, HAVELOCK. "Huysmans," in his <u>Affirmations</u>. Boston:
       Houghton Mifflin, pp. 158-211.
          Reprint of 1898.15.

2   SYMONS, ARTHUR. "Confessions: A Few Thoughts, Portraits and
       Memories." <u>Vanity Fair</u>, 5 (March), 39, 130.
          Reprint of a small portion of 1892.2. [Focus is on
       Huysmans' unique personality, his boredom with life, and
       his contempt for human imbecility.]

3   SYMONS, ARTHUR. "Joris-Karl Huysmans," in his <u>Figures of Sev</u>-
       <u>eral Centuries</u>. London: Constable, pp. 268-99.
          Reprint of 1892.2 with additions.
          Reprinted: 1918.4; 1969.22.

1917

1   BACOURT, PIERRE DE. "J.-K. Huysmans," in <u>Warner Library</u>.
       Vol. XIII. Edited by John W. Cunliffe and Ashley Thorndike.
       New York: Knickerbocker Press, 7834a-7834f.
          Discussion of Huysmans' life and books. "As a pure
       artist, as a master of words, he deserves our complete ad-
       miration." As an art critic, he showed rare instinctive
       knowledge. The painter's qualities, love and sense of
       color, keen judgment of value and masses are noticeable in
       every line he wrote. "Huysmans painted all his life, but
       he wielded a pen instead of a brush."

2   ELIOT, T. S. "The Borderline of Prose." <u>New Statesman</u>, 9
       (19 May), 157.
          Not fond of the Aesthetic Movement, Pater, or Huysmans,
       Eliot expressed a distaste for all three. "Time has left
       us many things, but amongst those it has taken away, we
       hope to count <u>A Rebours</u>." As for other "aesthetic eccen-
       tricities" of the Nineties, they, too, "may now be ignored."

1917

3   [HUNEKER, JAMES G.]. "J.-K. Huysmans--Genius of the Dis-
      agreeable." <u>Current Opinion</u>, 62 (March), 206.
         Huysmans pursued the disagreeable "with the ardor of a
      sportsman tracking game." Even Swift seems almost light and
      frolicsome by contrast. As a critic, Huysmans "vomited his
      contemporaries"; almost everything he wrote and said ran
      counter to accepted beliefs. Captious of virtually every-
      one and everything, he was as pitiless to himself as he was
      to others. Though he was the hero of all his novels, he
      was hardly a "lovable" one.
         Reprinted: 1917.4.

4   HUNEKER, JAMES G. "Opinions of J.-K. Huysmans," in his <u>Uni-
      corns</u>. New York: Scribner, pp. 111-20.
         Reprint of 1917.3.

5   MOORE, GEORGE. <u>Confessions of a Young Man</u>. New York:
      Brentano's.
         [<u>See</u> note appended to 1888.1.]

1918

1   BRENNEL, DOROTHEA. "Benson and Huysmans." <u>Month</u>, 132
      (December), 447-52.
         Comparative study of two authors who delved into reli-
      gious psychology. Both were converts to Roman Catholicism
      and devotees of mysticism. Benson, as a lover of nature,
      could find God in a fragrant garden. Huysmans preferred
      to seek Him "in some mighty fane of the Ages of Faith, to
      trace His Providence and plan in statues and moldings, in
      storied windows and vaulted roofs, in clustering shafts and
      towering pillars," as he did in <u>La Cathédrale</u>.

2   MOORE, GEORGE. <u>Confessions of a Young Man</u>. 4th ed. London:
      W. Heinemann.
         [<u>See</u> note appended to 1888.1.]

3   PAUL, KEGAN. "Translator's Note," in his translation of <u>En
      Route</u>. 4th ed. London: K. Paul, Trench, Trubner; New
      York: Dutton, pp. v-xi.
         Reprint of 1896.10.

4   SYMONS, ARTHUR. "Joris-Karl Huysmans," in his <u>Figures of Sev-
      eral Centuries</u>. London: Constable; New York: Dutton,
      pp. 268-99.
         Reprint of 1916.3.

5   SYMONS, ARTHUR. "The Decadent Movement in Literature." Lon-
        don Quarterly Review, 129 (January), 89-103.
            Reprint of 1893.2 with its last two paragraphs deleted.

1919

1   ANON. "En Route." Nation, 108 (24 May), 841.
            Review of Kegan Paul's translation of En Route: "a con-
        fession, exhaustive and exhausting in its prolix introspec-
        tive honesty--a confession which . . . recalls the tortured
        self-questioning of St. Augustine."

2   ANON. "En Route." New York Times, 24 (13 July), 369.
            Review of Kegan Paul's translation of En Route. This
        novel stands alone of its kind, "a treasure house of musi-
        cal criticism, a guide to hagiography, a passionate defense
        of mysticism, and withal one of the most sonorously splen-
        did compositions, from a purely literary point of view,
        that any language can boast." It will never appeal to a
        wide audience, but only to a select group of readers that
        many an author would give all his popularity to be able to
        hold.

3   D., W. "En Route." America, 21 (31 May), 208.
            Review of Kegan Paul's translation of En Route. Huys-
        mans' capable translator would have acted more prudently
        had he omitted the vivid descriptions of the penitent's
        anguish of soul before, during, and after the confession of
        his carnal sins. Such pages, however, as those treating of
        the liturgy and the contemplative life can scarcely be
        found anywhere else.

4   HUDSON, WILLIAM HENRY. A Short History of French Literature.
        London: G. Bell, p. 295.
            One of a group of young writers who gathered about Zola
        to form the School of Médan, Huysmans wrote fiction that
        was "heavy, unclear, bitterly pessimistic . . . which
        emphasized the creed of Naturalism at its worst." Then he
        became absorbed in the study of beauty; later, demonology
        and magic; finally, in mystical piety. All his interests
        are manifest in his novels.

5   REDFERN, MASON. "Huysmans and the Boulevard." Catholic
        World, 109 (June), 360-67.
            The boulevard has never quite forgiven Huysmans for his
        conversion, though many Parisians openly acknowledge his
        literary works. They remember him as an artificer of

1919

words, an erudite, sensitive artist; but they question
the sincerity of his books, especially En Route and La
Cathédrale.

6 SAINTSBURY, GEORGE. A History of the French Novel. Vol. II.
   London: Macmillan, 452, 453, 485, 515, 516, 574.
       The most remarkable of the Naturalists was probably
   Huysmans. His Les Soeurs Vatard is "a sort of apodiabo-
   losis of the Goncourts and Zola." A Rebours, which is
   really not a novel at all, is the history of Des Esseintes,
   who tried all arts and sensations: "his experiences being
   made by . . . a vehicle of mostly virulent and almost always worthless criticism on contemporaries." Later, Huysmans through "a cryptic and circuitous intention . . . took
   to the Black Arts; and at last he turned devout."

7 SYMONS, ARTHUR. "Joris-Karl Huysmans" and "The Later Huysmans"
   in his The Symbolist Movement in Literature. Revised and
   enlarged edition. New York: Dutton, pp. 230-61, 262-79.
       Reprint of 1892.2 and 1908.2.
       "The Later Huysmans" reprinted in 1958.9.

1920

1 FARNELL, FREDERICK J. "Erotism as Portrayed in Literature."
   International Journal of Psycho-Analysis, 1: 396-413.
       Includes a brief discussion of Huysmans as "one of the
   most distinctly repressive writers of the last century."
   His psycho-sexual personality dominated the greater part of
   his life. En Ménage, A Rebours, En Rade, Là-Bas, En Route,
   and La Cathédrale--each commented on from a psychoanalyti-
   cal point of view. In them, one can observe "a distinct
   pessimist with an exaggerated ego manifesting a homosexual
   component complemented by sadism and narcissism."

2 HUNEKER, JAMES G. Steeplejack. Vol. II. New York: Scrib-
   ners, 118-19.
       Writes of his correspondence with Huysmans in 1903 and
   his subsequent interview in Paris. Huysmans proved to be
   "a difficult man of gusty humours." Alludes to William
   James' abomination of the work of Huysmans, especially En
   Route. Notes that James later accepted the sincerity of
   Huysmans' life and art.

3 PAUL, KEGAN. "Translator's Note," in his translation of En
   Route. 4th ed. New York: Dutton, pp. v-xi.
       Reprint of 1896.10.

4   RASCOE, BURTON. "Painted Veils." <u>Chicago Daily News</u>
    (8 December), p. 13.
        Review of James G. Huneker's <u>Painted Veils</u> (New York:
    Boni & Liveright, 1920). Refers to the most sensational
    aspects of the book--the Holy Rollers incident and the
    banquet orgy--and Huneker's admission that they owed "some-
    thing to Huysmans' <u>Là-Bas</u> and <u>A Rebours</u> respectively."

5   RUDWIN, M. J. "The Satanism of Huysmans." <u>Open Court</u>, 34
    (April), 240-51.
        Traces Huysmans' flight from Naturalism into Decadence,
    where "he put up temporarily at a satanic half-way house."
    He had "a natural bent toward diabolism." A discussion of
    <u>Là-Bas</u> follows. Huysmans' presentation of medieval demon-
    ology and witchcraft was, on the whole, rather sound; but
    he is not "altogether trustworthy in regard to modern sa-
    tanism." His conversion was less a matter of choice than
    necessity. After he accepted Satan, he had to accept God.

6   WRIGHT, CUTHBERT. "The Real Huysmans." <u>Dial</u>, 69 (December),
    655-62.
        Covers Huysmans' early life and literary influences.
    Focuses briefly on <u>A Rebours</u> and <u>Là-Bas</u> as forerunners of
    "the ultimate step in his pilgrimage." Huysmans wrote some
    extraordinary works "in a chiselled and jewelled prose,
    some of which will endure." In many respects, <u>En Route</u> is
    his best book.

<u>1921</u>

1   ANON. "New Books." <u>Catholic World</u>, 112 (January), 552.
        Review of Kegan Paul's translation of <u>En Route</u>: "stands
    very well that most searching test of literary merit, a
    careful rereading. Few modern novels can pass through this
    ordeal successfully."

2   BLUNT, H. F. "J.-K. Huysmans," in his <u>Great Penitents</u>. New
    York: Macmillan, pp. 169-90.
        Huysmans was an individual "who plumbed the depths of
    iniquity and who afterwards aimed at the peaks of sancti-
    ty." During his early years as a writer there was nothing
    of any value but Naturalism; but later, sick of physical
    and moral degeneracy, he wrote <u>A Rebours</u>, a novel in which
    he sought after something more. Led by what he dubbed
    "extraordinary ways," he came to embrace Catholicism. As
    a convert, he put his literary talent to work in <u>En Route</u>,

1921

La Cathédrale, and L'Oblat. When he died on May 12, 1907, he was buried, as he had requested, in the robe of a Bene- dictine monk.
Reprinted: 1967.2.

3   ELLIS, HAVELOCK. "Huysmans," in his The New Spirit. New York: Boni & Liveright, pp. 219-70.
Reprint of 1898.15.

4   GOURMONT, REMY DE. "Huysmans," in his Book of Masks. Trans- lated by Jack Lewis. Boston: Luce, pp. 195-201.
Collection of comments on some fifty poets, novelists, and intellectuals, among whom is Huysmans. As an author, Huysmans saw life as no other person has ever seen it, for "no one was ever gifted with a glance so sharp, so boring. . . . Huysmans is an eye."
Reprinted: 1967.9.

5   HUNEKER, JAMES G. "Pessimist's Progress: J.-K. Huysmans," in his Egoists: A Book of Supermen. New York: Scribner, pp. 167-206.
Reprint of 1907.13.

6   SHUSTER, GEORGE. "Joris-Karl Huysmans: Egoist and Mystic." Catholic World, 113 (July), 452-64.
An egoist for whom nothing in life had permanent value, Huysmans had an eye of microscopic power that viewed the world in a totally individual way. His attitude toward women, his asceticism, and his lack of democratic sympathy or brotherly love are all ear-marks of his egoism.

1922

1   ANON. "The Character of Huysmans." Times Literary Supple- ment, no.1,044 (19 January), p. 40.
Huysmans' books are best explained by a description of his personality rather than by an impersonal analysis of his work. His temperament was that of the satirist; it was impossible for him to see persons and things except in their worst and most ridiculous light. The average man seeks to rid himself of boredom through banal methods, but Huysmans sought distraction in constantly renewed novelties of aesthetic stimulation.

2   ELLIS, HAVELOCK. "Huysmans," in his Affirmations. Boston and New York: Houghton Mifflin; London: Constable, pp. 158-211.
Reprint of 1898.15.

3   ELLIS, HAVELOCK.   Introduction to John Howard's translation of
    A Rebours. New York: Lieber & Lewis, pp. v-viii.
        Reprint of 1898.15 in abbreviated form.

4   GEDDES, VIRGIL. "Huysmans, Trappist and Litterateur." Poet
    Lore, 33 (Winter), 521-24.
        Huysmans' retreat to a Trappist monastery is a good ex-
    ample of the seriousness of his character. He sought "a
    release from the world's stupid, incessant habit of action
    without significance, from the world's desuetude of mental
    and spiritual inaction." And he remains perhaps the most
    important fictional chronicler of "that vast and beautiful
    epoch of intellectual energy known . . . as the French
    decadence."

5   HUNEKER, JAMES G. Overtones: A Book of Temperaments. New
    York: Scribner, pp. 204-10.
        Reprint of 1904.2.

6   JACKSON, HOLBROOK. The Eighteen Nineties: A Review of Art
    and Ideas at the Close of the Nineteenth Century. London:
    Grant Richards; New York: Knopf, pp. 28, 58, 61, 63, 136,
    223.
        Reprint of 1913.2.

7   PAUL, KEGAN. Prefatory note to Clara Bell's translation of
    La Cathédrale. London: K. Paul, Trench, Trubner,
    pp. vii-xi.
        Reprint of 1898.16.

1923

1   ANON. "New Books: The Cathedral." Catholic World, 117
    (June), 427-28.
        A review of Clara Bell's translation of La Cathédrale.
    Huysmans' entire outlook changed with a visit he made to a
    Trappist monastery at Issigny in 1895. His interest in
    religion led him to Chartres; here he studied the Gothic
    ideal as found in stone and carvings. The result is this
    novel.

2   ANON. "New Books: St. Lydwine of Schiedam." Catholic World,
    118 (October), 135-36.
        Review of Agnes Hastings' translation of Sainte Lydwine
    de Schiedam. This biography of a Dutch saint is deftly
    drawn, but in a realism that borders on the grotesque.
    Huysmans did not save his portrait--as a Rembrandt would

1923

have done--by blotting out superfluous details. In spite
of its artistry, Huysmans' portrait of St. Lydwine is
repulsive.

3   ANON. "Saint Lydwine." Spectator, 130 (26 May), 892.
Review of Agnes Hastings' translation of Sainte Lydwine
de Schiedam. The interest of this book is not limited to
the devout and the literary. Significant is the glimpse it
gives into the mental life of the fourteenth century, "when
the supernatural was the most natural thing in the world."

4   BACOURT, PIERRE DE and J. W. CUNLIFFE. French Literature During the Last Half-Century. New York: Macmillan, pp. 20,
35, 45, 253, 264-65.
Huysmans was one of the Circle of Five who gathered
around Zola early in their careers; the others were Guy de
Maupassant, Léon Hennique, Paul Alexis, and Henry Céard.
When Symbolism began to attract attention in 1885, it was
not, as Huysmans suggested, "a joke invented by Anatole
France to vex the Parnassians." One of the greatest of the
Symbolists, as it turned out, was Mallarmé; but he was vir-
tually unknown until Huysmans adulated him in A Rebours.

5   BUTLER, KATHLEEN T. A History of French Literature. Vol. II.
New York: Dutton, 239, 319, 320.
After writing a series of novels "in which he outdid
Zola in minute and uncompromising naturalism," Huysmans
turned to literary and artistic symbolism. The most famous
of his novels, La Cathédrale, is an interpretation of the
symbolism of Chartres; in it he "shows how inert matter,
how stone, wood, and glass may acquire through symbol a
spiritual significance."
Reprinted: 1966.5.

6   CRANE, CLARKSON. "Twenty Years After." Freeman, 6 (10 January), 428.
Review of John Howard's translation of A Rebours: "a
curious, ridiculous and puerile book which few spirits will
always cherish with an indulgent and amused affection."

7   ELLIS, HAVELOCK. Introduction to John Howard's translation of
A Rebours. New York: Boni, pp. v-viii.
Reprint of 1898.15 in abbreviated form.

8   HUTTON, W. H. "The Cathedral in Fiction." Quarterly Review,
239 (April), 336-49.
Discussion of three books, one of which is La Cathédrale. There is no better guide to the great church of

1923

Chartres than Huysmans' novel; moreover, this novel recommends faith, steadfastness, rest in God.

9 JACKSON, HOLBROOK. The Eighteen Nineties: A Review of Art and Ideas at the Close of the Nineteenth Century. New York: Knopf, pp. 28, 58, 61, 136, 223.
       Reprint of 1913.2.

10 LE B., F. P. "Saint Lydwine of Schiedam." America, 29 (4 August), 378.
       Review of Agnes Hastings' translation of Sainte Lydwine de Schiedam: "an edifying biography of a fourteenth-century stigmatic and leading exponent of the mystical doctrine of substitution."

11 LOVING, PIERRE. "Huysmans for the Disenchanted." Nation, 116 (10 January), 44-45.
       Review of John Howard's translation of A Rebours: "a significant book because it voices the invalidism of life with insight and precision; it is beautiful and spotted just as Huysmans' soul was beautiful and spotted. It condenses not only the introverted man, but the neurasthenic age in which he lived."

12 MOORE, GEORGE. Confessions of a Young Man. New York: Boni & Liveright.
       [See note appended to 1888.1.]

13 R., J. E. "St. Lydwine." New Statesman, 21 (28 April), 86-88.
       Review of Agnes Hastings' translation of Sainte Lydwine de Schiedam. Though not one of his more important books, this study shows that Huysmans was not "a tepid hagiographer."

14 WESTCOTT, GLENWAY. "A Rebours." Literary Review of the New York Evening Post, 3 (9 December), 292.
       Review of John Howard's translation of A Rebours. The trappings of romance have "overlaid and obscured the story and weakened whatever emotions are proper to it."

15 WRIGHT, CUTHBERT. "The Snows of Yesterday." Dial, 74 (March), 303-306.
       Review of John Howard's translation of A Rebours: "a very precious and remarkable work." The translation, however, "must have been a labor of love."

1924

1924

1 ANON. "The Oblat." <u>Times Literary Supplement</u>, no. 1,168
       (5 June), p. 357.
           Review of Edward Perceval's translation of <u>L'Oblat</u>.
       "The looseness of the translation . . . destroys . . . the
       individuality of Huysmans' style and mind." A thorough re-
       vision is needed.

2 ELLIS, HAVELOCK. "Huysmans," in his <u>Affirmations</u>. Boston:
       Houghton Mifflin, pp. 158-211.
           Reprint of 1898.15.

3 ELLIS, HAVELOCK. Introduction to John Howard's translation
       of <u>A Rebours</u>. New York: Boni, pp. v-viii.
           Reprint of 1898.15 in abbreviated form.

4 GILMORE, LOUIS. "Reviews." <u>Double Dealer</u>, 7 (November-
       December), 77-79.
           Review of 1924 English publication of <u>Là-Bas</u>: "marvel-
       lous narrative . . . superb drama."

5 HUNEKER, JAMES G. "Pessimist's Progress: J.-K. Huysmans,"
       in his <u>Egoists: A Book of Supermen</u>. New York: Scribner,
       pp. 167-206.
           Reprint of 1907.13.

6 KRUTCH, JOSEPH W. "Making Good." <u>Nation</u>, 119 (26 November),
       575-76.
           Review of Edward Perceval's translation of <u>L'Oblat</u>.
       The least interesting of the tetralogy of which <u>Là-Bas</u> is
       the first volume, but "to those who, like the present re-
       viewer, find the author-hero strangely fascinating, it is
       certainly not dull."

7 LALOU, RENÉ. <u>Contemporary French Literature</u>. New York:
       Knopf, pp. 44-45.
           Huysmans' style always saves everything he writes from
       mediocrity: "Violent, loaded with material details, with
       sudden sarcastic outbursts, it always remains equally
       imaginative."

8 MUNSON, G. B. "The Oblate." <u>Literary Review of the New York
       Evening Post</u>, 4 (27 September), 4.
           Review of Edward Perceval's translation of <u>L'Oblat</u>.
       Huysmans evolved "a complex, sometimes tortured, but always
       scintillating and encrusted style." In this novel it would
       appear that he has worked toward a simpler and clearer

method of expression. It is a pity that the translator
"lacked the resources to convey fully . . . the flavor of
Huysmans' style."

9   S., H. "Huysmans' Past." New York World (24 August), Sec. 4,
    p. 8.
        Review of Edward Perceval's translation of L'Oblat.
    "If Huysmans is an artist he must be ashamed of this book,
    written apparently during his literary novitiate. If it
    were not Huysmans, it would not have been translated."

10 SYMONS, ARTHUR. "The Later Huysmans," in his Collected Works.
    Vol. VIII. London: Martin Secker, 187-97.
        Reprint of 1908.2.

11 TINKER, EDWARD L. Lafcadio Hearn's American Days. New York:
    Dodd, Mead, p. 113.
        In some of his journalistic work Hearn gives evidence of
    being influenced by Huysmans' own special brand of medie-
    valism.
        Reprinted: 1925.7.

1925

1   JACKSON, HOLBROOK. The Eighteen Nineties: A Review of Art
    and Ideas at the Close of the Nineteenth Century. New
    York: Knopf, pp. 28, 58, 61, 63, 136, 223.
        Reprint of 1913.2.

2   KASTNER, L. E. and HENRY GIBSON ATKINS. A Short History of
    French Literature. New York: Holt, pp. 321-22.
        Biographical-critical entry. "As a stylist Huysmans is
    occasionally powerful, but more often heavy and truculent."
        Reprinted: 1970.10.

3   McMAHON, J. H. "Our Lady's Greatest Shrine." Catholic World,
    121 (September), 749-55.
        Review-article on W. H. Mitchell's translation of Les
    Foules de Lourdes: "One of the most valuable books written
    about Lourdes."

4   MITCHELL, W. H. Preface to his translation of Les Foules de
    Lourdes. London: Burns Oates, pp. v-viii.
        Affords a good insight into Huysmans himself. At times
    too caustic about what he saw at the Shrine, its debased
    art and commercial atmosphere, he weakens his case through
    bias and extravagance. His prejudices and antipathies,

1925

    nevertheless, serve to accentuate his primary purpose in
writing this work. Despite his distaste for the hustle of
the multitude, he meant his last book to be "a whole-
hearted tribute to Our Lady of Lourdes."

5   PAUL, KEGAN. Prefatory note to Clara Bell's translation of La
    Cathédrale. New York: Dutton, pp. vii-xi.
        Reprint of 1898.16.

6   ROBINSON, LANDON M. "The Crowds of Lourdes." Commonweal, 2
    (24 June), 193.
        Review of W. H. Mitchell's translation of Les Foules de
    Lourdes. In response to Zola's attack on Lourdes, Huysmans
went there and wrote this touching and eloquent defense.
He mingled with the throngs and responded to human suffering. A sympathetic and vivid journalist, he produced more
of a diary than an impersonal work of art.

7   TINKER, EDWARD L. Lafcadio Hearn's American Days. London:
    Bodley Head, p. 113.
        Reprint of 1924.11.

1926

1   ELLIS, HAVELOCK. "Huysmans," in his Affirmations. Boston and
    New York: Houghton Mifflin; London: Constable,
    pp. 158-211.
        Reprint of 1898.15.

2   ELLIS, HAVELOCK. Introduction to John Howard's translation of
    A Rebours. New York: Boni, pp. v-viii.
        Reprint of 1898.15 in abbreviated form.

3   MOORE, GEORGE. Confessions of a Young Man. New and revised
    edition. London: W. Heinemann.
        [See note appended to 1888.1.]

4   WRIGHT, C. H. C. The Background of Modern French Literature.
    New York: Ginn & Co., pp. 9, 156, 234, 243, 273, 279, 297,
    302.
        In Huysmans' early novels, there is "an ironic nihilism,
morbid and neurotic dilettantism and satanism"; later he
"dabbled in the aesthetic side of Catholicism."

1   JACKSON, HOLBROOK. <u>The Eighteen Nineties: A Review of Art
    and Ideas at the Close of the Nineteenth Century</u>. New
    York: Knopf, pp. 28, 58, 61, 63, 136, 223.
        Reprint of 1913.2.

2   PUTNAM, SAMUEL. Preface to his translation of <u>A Vau-l'Eau</u>.
    Chicago: Covici, pp. ix-xvi.
        Explains the make-up of this volume; the works selected
    for inclusion are meant to round out a view of the man and
    the writer. Both M. Folatin of <u>A Vau-l'Eau</u> and the title
    character of <u>Marthe</u> drift constantly, hopelessly down-
    stream. "Each goes, inevitably, from bad to worse. Each
    is a study, strikingly modern in vividness and approach,
    of the disintegration of a human soul." Selections from
    <u>Le Drageoir à épices</u>, <u>Certains</u>, and <u>L'Art moderne</u> further
    help to understand the young Huysmans.
        Reprinted: 1975.12.

3   ROOSBROECK, G. L. VAN. "Huysmans the Sphinx: The Riddle of
    <u>A Rebours</u>." <u>Romanic Review</u>, 18 (October-December), 306-28.
        Discussion of <u>A Rebours</u> as "one of the most vilified as
    well as one of the most glorified books in modern litera-
    ture." Purports a riddle is solved by reading the novel
    as "a caricature of the poets of '85" and as an "obvious
    parody of Decadence." The reader must be aware of the
    "moral imbecility of Des Esseintes, his improbable neuro-
    sis, his strange experiments and sensuous perversions."
        Reprinted: 1927.4.

4   ROOSBROECK, G. L. VAN. "Huysmans the Sphinx: The Riddle of
    <u>A Rebours</u>," in his <u>The Riddle of the Decadents</u>. New York:
    Columbia Univ., The French Institute, pp. 40-71.
        Reprint of 1927.3.

1   HUDDLESTON, SISLEY. "Whitewashing Bluebeard," in his <u>Articles
    de Paris</u>. New York: Macmillan, pp. 92-95.
        Discussion of Gilles de Rais as portrayed in <u>Là-Bas</u>.
    Huysmans suggests in his novel that "the religious exalta-
    tion which Gilles de Rais experienced in his Joan of Arc
    days was converted into a mystical sadism and satanism."

2   HUNEKER, JAMES G. <u>Overtones: A Book of Temperaments</u>. New
    York: Scribner, pp. 204-10.
        Reprint of 1904.2.

1928

3 JORGENSEN, JOHANNES. <u>An Autobiography</u>. Translated by Inge-
   borg Lund. London: Sheed & Ward. Vol. 1: pp. 142, 144,
   145, 265; Vol. II: pp. 35, 39, 34, 335-36, 354-55.
       Inspired and influenced by Huysmans. Agreed with Des
   Esseintes and Durtal that modern culture was at a low ebb.
   Jorgensen's <u>Le Livre de la Route</u> took its title and origin
   from Huysmans' <u>En Route</u>.

4 JOSEPHSON, MATTHEW. <u>Zola and His Time</u>. New York: Garden
   City Publishing Co.; London: Gollancz, pp. 222, 224, 225,
   240, 260, 265, 266, 268-72, 283, 286, 309, 317, 355, 357,
   358, 383.
       In 1871, after reading Zola's novels for a few years,
   Huysmans determined to visit his literary hero. He did so
   through Henry Céard. A friendship developed between Huysmans and Zola. When Huysmans completed <u>Les Soeurs Vatard</u>,
   Zola had Charpentier publish it, telling the publisher that
   "Huysmans was the novelist of tomorrow." Huysmans dedicated the book to the Master of Médan, who, in a review,
   called it "a book of combat . . . with an intense life,
   which arouses the most provoking questions." In 1880,
   Huysmans, along with Zola's other young disciples Hennique,
   Céard, Maupassant, and Alexis, contributed to a collection
   of short stories on the Franco-Prussian War. Huysmans'
   story was "Sac au dos." The title of the volume, Huysmans suggested, should be "The Comic Invasion," but the
   others decided <u>Les Soirées de Médan</u> would be a way of rendering honor to Zola. In 1884, Huysmans broke with Zola
   over the publication of <u>A Rebours</u>. Zola reproached Huysmans for "delivering a terrible blow to Naturalism." Huysmans maintained that he had "liberated" literature.
       Reprinted: 1932.3; 1969.14.

5 MOORE, GEORGE. <u>Confessions of a Young Man</u>. 5th ed. London:
   Heinemann.
       [<u>See</u> note appended to 1888.1.]

6 THURSTAN, F. "Huysmans' Excursion into Occultism." <u>Occult
   Review</u>, 48 (October), 227-36.
       In the 1880's, as we know from Huysmans' diaries, he
   witnessed some extraordinary events at séances to which he
   got himself invited. On different occasions he beheld all
   sorts of revenants, veridical or simulated. He became a
   believer in spirit reality and devoured books on magic and
   the occult. In 1889, he met Abbé Boullan; discussions and
   research into satanism and black magic resulted in <u>Là-Bas</u>.
   It also resulted in Huysmans' denunciation of a secret society in Paris, the Society of the Cabalistic Red Cross,
   and a challenge to a duel by the offended leader of that

Society, Count Stanilas de Guaita. The duel never came off. Shortly thereafter, the materialist Huysmans converted to the Church, "turned mystic," and devoted his time almost exclusively "to mystical art and mystical poesy."

1929

1   ELLIS, HAVELOCK. "Huysmans," in his Affirmations. London:
     Constable, pp. 158-211.
        Reprint of 1898.15.

2   GUERQUIN, PIERRE. "Un Portrait de J.-K. Huysmans by Forain."
     Revue de l'Art, 56 (September), 170-72.
        [English summary of this article appears in a supplement.] Forain painted a portrait of Huysmans in 1878.
     Upon Huysmans' death, the portrait passed to Henry Girard.
     Subsequently it was purchased by the Curator of the Versailles Museum.

3   HUNEKER, JAMES G. "Pessimist's Progress: J.-K. Huysmans,"
     in his Essays. New York: Scribner, pp. 247-76.
        Reprint of 1907.13.

4   LAVRIN, JANKO. "Huysmans and Strindberg," in his Studies in
     European Literature. London: Constable, pp. 118-30.
        Recounts basic facts of Huysmans' life and dilates upon
     his books. States that Strindberg read En Route in 1897
     and commented on it in his autobiographic Legends: "Huysmans may go to the Trappists and confess to the priest; for
     my part . . . it is enough that my sin be publicly acknowledged in writing." Strindberg's fate, however, was analogous to that of Huysmans'. A discussion of Strindberg's
     life and works follows. The writings of both writers "are
     an eloquent expression of the modern spiritual crisis, in
     so far as that can be reflected in literature." Huysmans
     and Strindberg were both "tragic wrestlers for a fuller
     inner life."
        Reprinted: 1970.11.

5   MOORE, GEORGE. Confessions of a Young Man. London: Heinemann.
        [See note appended to 1888.1.]

6   OLIVERO, F. "Joris-Karl Huysmans as Poet." Poetry Review,
     20 (July), 237-46.
        Discusses the "poetical elements of Huysmans' prose."
     Because of the originality and lyric quality of his style,
     his prose is a texture of metaphors, images, personifica-

1929

    tions, and symbols akin to poetry. His whole work may be
    considered as "in a poem of the soul, a lyrical manifesta-
    tion in prose, like The Pilgrim's Progress."

7   RAYBOULD, A. "The Cathedral." Catholic World, 128 (January),
    443-48.
        To Huysmans the symbolist, Chartres Cathedral was "the
    open book of the Middle Ages." To read that book best one
    should read his novel The Cathedral.

1930

1   DESCAVES, LUCIEN. Introduction to Down There. London:
    Fortune Press, pp. v-xi.
        Gives brief biography of Huysmans and refers to his most
    important books. Of them all, "Là-Bas is the one that
    caused Huysmans the most vexations." Because much of the
    novel came from actual research he conducted among Parisian
    demonologists, they "declared war on him for revealing mat-
    ters that should have remained in the arcana of modern
    Satanism." To ex-Abbé Boullan, Huysmans wrote: "I give
    you my word that my book will be a bombshell in that camp."
    It is doubtful that Huysmans ever attended a Black Mass
    similar to those described in Là-Bas.

2   ELLIS, HAVELOCK. "Huysmans," in his The New Spirit. New
    York: Modern Library, pp. 219-70.
        Reprint of 1898.15.

3   ELLIS, HAVELOCK. Introduction to John Howard's translation
    of A Rebours. New York: Modern Library; Toronto: McLeod,
    pp. v-viii.
        Reprint of 1898.15 in abbreviated form.

4   SMITH, A. C. "The Language of J.-K. Huysmans." Doctoral dis-
    sertation, London University.

5   VERCADE, WILLIBRORD DOM. Yesterdays of an Artist-Monk.
    Translated by John L. Stoddard. New York: P. J. Kennedy,
    pp. 53-55, 106.
        Among the most important books Vercade read as a young
    man were Tolstoi's My Confessions and Huysmans' A Rebours.
    From Tolstoi, Vercade learned there was something higher
    and more consoling than art. From Huysmans, he perceived
    the degeneracy that shows in many painters and poets at the
    beginning of their twenties. Though often suspicious of
    Huysmans, A Rebours, which he read with "genuine delight,"
    forced him to think about life, society, art, and religion.

1931

1   ADDLESHAW, S. "French Novel and the Catholic Church." Church
     Quarterly Review, 112 (April), 65-87.
         Discussion of Huysmans' literary career. With A Rebours,
     Huysmans started on a new path. Là-Bas indicates his spir-
     itual progress, despite its "appalling account of the blas-
     phemies of the Black Mass and Satan Worship." The story of
     the conquest of his sensual nature continues in En Route,
     La Cathédrale and L'Oblat; there is nothing in English with
     which to compare these three great religious novels.

2   ELLIS, HAVELOCK. Introduction to John Howard's translation of
     A Rebours. New York: Hartsdale House; New York: Three
     Sirens, pp. 11-49.
         Reprint of 1898.15.

3   GREEN, FREDERICK C. French Novelists: From the Revolution to
     Proust. London: J. M. Dent, pp. 286, 287-88, 298, 304.
         En Ménage is "a variant of the Education sentimentale
     . . . but Huysmans lacks Flaubert's genius for the truly
     significant trait." Huysmans drifted from Naturalism by
     way of Satanism into "a wooly and mystic Catholicism."
     Reprinted: 1964.2.

4   HANIGHAN, FRANK C. "Across Huysmans' Paris." Commonweal, 13
     (18 March), 45-46.
         Compares the Paris of 1931 with the Paris of Huysmans'
     time. Huysmans' castigation of religious and non-religious
     monuments was severe. Only at St. Séverin or St. Sulpice
     did he find refuge; at these churches he listened to plain-
     chant, which he found one of the glories of Catholicism.

5   HANIGHAN, FRANK C. "Huysmans' Conversion." Open Court, 45
     (August), 474-81.
         Discussion of attacks that impugned Huysmans' spiritual
     sincerity from cynics, Freudians, Catholics, and others.
     He was not "an academic advocate of the Catholicism of
     medieval times." Possibly Huysmans failed to observe all
     the teachings of the Sermon on the Mount, but this hardly
     alters the fact that his was "a sincere conversion."

6   HANSEN, HARRY. Mid-West Portraits: A Book of Memories and
     Friendships. New York: Harcourt, Brace, pp. 311-12.
         Relates Ben Hecht's love for Huysmans. Hecht, who read
     En Route and La Cathédrale in translation, sat night after
     night with an obliging friend who sight-translated Là-Bas
     for him. In contrast to Huysmans, American writers seemed
     tame and colorless. It was Hecht's opinion that Huysmans

1931

was "the rajah of writing, his brain the splendid macaw of literatures." Huysmans' work, "from beginning to end a fulgurating panorama of phrases, forms the rarest and most precious pages in the thought of France." All stylists would have to be compared to him: "Huysmans' decadence is the most virile and furious manifestation of beauty in any language."

7 HUTSON, DALE DELOIN. "The Influence of the Works of Joris-Karl Huysmans on the Later Works of George Moore." Master's thesis, Ohio State University.

8 JACKSON, HOLBROOK. The Eighteen Nineties: A Review of Art and Ideas at the Close of the Nineteenth Century. London: J. Cape, pp. 28, 58, 61, 63, 136, 223.
    Reprint of 1913.2.

9 RABE, ELIZABETH V. "Huysmans, the Art Critic." Master's thesis, Columbia University.

10 ROTHENSTEIN, WILLIAM. Men and Memories, 1872-1900. Vol. I. New York: Coward McCann, 138-39.
    Pater had a habit of often assuming ignorance on subjects about which he was well-informed. "He questions me closely about Mallarmé and Verlaine, Huysmans and de Goncourt."

11 WEST, NATHANAEL. The Dream Life of Balso Snell. Paris & New York: Contact Editions, pp. 34-36.
    [One character in this novel, a surrealist fantasy, is writing a biography of Samuel Perkins: Smeller, a man whose nose dominated his other senses to such an extent that it was his only point of communication with the world. West was influenced by "Les Similitudes" and "Le Gousset," two prose poems from Croquis parisiens, in which Huysmans dwells upon synaesthesia and the sense of smell. In a clever parody that runs several paragraphs, West has Perkins "able to translate the sensations, sound, sight, taste, and touch, into that of smell. He could smell a chord in D minor . . . the caress of velvet . . . the strength of iron . . . an isosceles triangle. . . . He had found in the odors of a woman's body . . . a world of dreams, seas, forests, textures, colors, flavors, forms. . . ."]

12   WILSON, EDMUND. <u>Axel's Castle: A Study in the Imaginative</u>
      <u>Literature of 1870-1930</u>. New York: Scribner's, pp. 10,
      18, 48, 49, 94, 264-65, 267.
            Various allusions to Huysmans and comments on Des Es-
      seintes, "who set the fashion for so many other personali-
      ties, fictitious and real, at the end of the century."
      Discusses Des Esseintes' desire to see London after being
      "excited by the novels of Dickens"; but after "driving
      through a fog in Paris, visiting Galignani's English book-
      store, dining at an English restaurant . . . it occurs to
      him how disappointed he had been by a visit to Holland.
      The real London, he concludes, cannot possibly come up to
      one he has been imagining, so he returns to Fontenay, where
      he can exist isolated and insulated from the world."
            Reprinted: 1959.12; 1961.11.

1932

1   BARBUSSE, HENRI. <u>Zola</u>. Translated by Mary B. Green and
      Frederick C. Green. London: J. M. Dent, pp. 106, 107,
      120, 133, 137, 138-45, 158, 161, 172, 180, 193, 205, 207,
      209-11, 219.
            Relates how Huysmans, Céard, Hennique, Alexis, and Mau-
      passant decided to contribute each a short story to <u>Les</u>
      <u>Soirées de Médan</u> (1880); and then how over the years each
      of these disciples of Zola drifted away. Huysmans, who was
      "lovesick for beauty," did so in 1884 with <u>A Rebours</u>, con-
      vinced that the Naturalistic formula of Zola had exhausted
      itself.

2   HUNEKER, JAMES G. "Pessimist's Progress: J.-K. Huysmans, "
      in his <u>Egoists: A Book of Supermen</u>. New York: Scribner,
      pp. 167-206.
            Reprint of 1907.13.

3   JOSEPHSON, MATTHEW. Zola and His Time. New York: Garden
      City Publishing Co., pp. 222, 224, 225, 240, 260, 265, 266,
      268-72, 283, 286, 309, 317, 355, 357, 358, 383.
            Reprint of 1928.4.

4   SUMMERS, MONTAGUE. "J.-K. Huysmans and the Cathedral of
      Chartres." <u>Architectural Design and Construction</u>, 3
      (November), 10-13.
            When Huysmans was writing <u>La Cathédrale</u>, he remarked
      that because of its architectural technicalities he feared
      it would prove "absolutely unreadable." But such was not

1933

the case, the book going into more than thirty editions.
Despite its excessive documentation, La Cathédrale is,
indeed, unique: "an epic of ecclesiastical architecture."

1933

1 COLUCCI, FRANK. "Joris-Karl Huysmans' Art Criticism." Doctoral dissertation, Cornell University.

2 HANIGHAN, FRANK C. "Huysmans' Influence in America." Revue
de littérature comparée (Année 13), 173-86.
Traces some of the first translations of Huysmans' works
into English and discusses their reception in America.
Quotes from and alludes to reactions of Harry Thurston
Peck, James G. Huneker, Carl Van Vechten, Edgar Saltus, Ben
Hecht, and others. Gives figures on sales of translations,
which are "impressive enough to indicate that Huysmans has
a considerable reading public in America."

3 MARCHAND, HENRY L. The Erotic History of France. New York:
Privately printed [Panurge Press], pp. 253, 255-57.
Brief discussion of Là-Bas as a novel in which its hero
is "persecuted by erotic spectres . . . obsessed by saty-
riasis." But as an eroticist, Huysmans was "strictly
limited."

4 MOORE, GEORGE. Confessions of a Young Man. London: Heinemann.
[See note appended to 1888.1.]

5 PRAZ, MARIO. Romantic Agony. Translated by Angus Davidson.
London: Oxford Univ. Press, pp. 133, 267, 268, 291,
292-94, 296, 303, 305-12, 321, 338, 340, 347, 351-53, 369,
374, 380, 382, 390, 391, 398, 405, 406, 409, 426.
Discusses A Rebours; labels the novel "the pivot upon
which the whole psychology of the Decadent Movement turns
. . . all the prose works of the Decadence, from Lorrain
to Gourmont, Wilde and D'Annunzio, are contained in embryo
in A Rebours." Explains its descent from Baudelaire.
Notes Huysmans' interest in the art of Gustave Moreau and
Félicien Rops, the literature of Mallarmé and Poe. Focuses, in an exposition on the Fatal Woman, on Hyacinthe of
Là-Bas, who initiates Durtal into the Black Mass. Traces
the aesthetic ancestry of Wilde's Dorian Gray "mainly to
Mademoiselle de Maupin and A Rebours."
Reprinted: 1951.7; 1970.16 in slightly revised
editions.

1934

1 BRENNEN, JOSEPH G. "Joris-Karl Huysmans." Catholic World,
40 (December), 323-31.
Although an outstanding figure in the history of French
prose, Huysmans is too consistently neglected by contemporary critics. In his masterpiece A Rebours the main character, Des Esseintes, is Huysmans himself. This autobiographical factor is continued in Là-Bas, En Route, La
Cathédrale, and L'Oblat, where once again the central
figure, Durtal, is a masked figure of the author himself.
A unique man of letters, Huysmans in his fiction presents
a thoroughly personal artistic view of the world, but one
that is not easily accepted by those who read him.

2 JACKSON, HOLBROOK. The Eighteen Nineties: A Review of Art
and Ideas at the Close of the Nineteenth Century. London:
J. Cape, pp. 28, 58, 61, 63, 136, 223.
Reprint of 1913.2.

3 STEWARD, S. M. "J.-K. Huysmans and George Moore." Romanic
Review, 25 (July), 197-206.
In Drama in Muslin, Moore mingles with his recounting of
bourgeois life heavy and laborious imitations of Huysmans.
In A Mere Accident, Moore, under the direct influence of A
Rebours, presents a pale copy of Des Esseintes. In Mike
Fletcher, the stylistic qualities of the lengthy monologues,
the abundance of paradox, and the brilliant texture of
metaphor recall a rather febrile Huysmans. Moore gained
from Huysmans an interest in Aestheticism, the technique of
spiritual naturalism, and an unusual avenue of metaphor.

1935

1 BAISIER, LEON. "Joris-Karl Huysmans--His Varied Career."
Sign, 15 (December), 273-74.
Huysmans' literary life can be divided into three pe-
riods. Marthe, Les Soeurs Vatard, and En Ménage mark his
first period; A Rebours and Là-Bas, the second; and En
Route, La Cathédrale and L'Oblat, the third. In the first
period, he opposed the spirit of Romanticism. The second
stage is transitional and was one during which he sought
beauty and truth. His final period demonstrates a movement
toward mysticism and the liturgy.

1935

2   ELLIS, HAVELOCK. <u>From Rousseau to Proust</u>. Boston: Houghton
       Mifflin, pp. 5, 11-13, 174, 269, 313, 324, 380, 394.
          Discusses Huysmans' personality: "finely strung na-
       ture"; "tended to be dyspeptic" yet he had "tender humanity
       and boundless charity." His appearance suggested an air of
       refined distinction. "When I look back, Huysmans remains
       for me, of all the men I have ever known, perhaps the most
       unalloyed embodiment of genius." As a writer, he influ-
       enced the early work of Remy de Gourmont. Huysmans' lit-
       erary ability was akin to that of Proust. "The angle at
       which Huysmans viewed the world often tended to make the
       noraml appear abnormal, while Proust's vision tended to
       make the abnormal more normal. . . ."
          Reprinted: 1936.1; 1968.2.

3   ELLIS, HAVELOCK. "Huysmans," in his <u>The New Spirit</u>. Washing-
       ton, D.C.: National Home Library Foundation, pp. 219-70.
          Reprint of 1898.15.

4   McAGHON, ARTHUR D. "Books--and a Book." <u>America</u>, 52
       (9 March), 518-19.
          A certain individual claimed that he came to appreciate
       the mysteries of Catholicism through reading <u>En Route</u>, but
       only in the official missal of the Church did he find a
       proper understanding of the liturgical cycle.

5   MacCARTHY, DESMOND. <u>Experience</u>. New York: Oxford Univ.
       Press, pp. 295-96.
          Possibly there is little greatness of mind in the in-
       dictment of life found in Huysmans' books, but his Natur-
       alistic novels provide a peculiar pleasure: "The fun of
       reading Huysmans is the fun of seeing the ugly, dank, flac-
       cid thing presented not as it is, but even uglier, greas-
       ier, meaner."

1936

1   ELLIS, HAVELOCK. <u>From Rousseau to Proust</u>. London: Consta-
       ble, pp. 5, 11-13, 174, 269, 313, 324, 380, 394.
          Reprint of 1935.2.

2   FORSTER, E. M. <u>Abinger Harvest</u>. London: Edward Arnold; New
       York: Harcourt, Brace, pp. 90, 106.
          Alludes to authors he read during the madness of World
       War I, especially "those who had nothing tangible to of-
       fer: Blake, William Morris, the early T. S. Eliot, J.-K.
       Huysmans, Yeats." He read whatever was the least likely
       to be bracing. "Huysmans' <u>A Rebours</u> is the book of that

period that I remember best. Oh, the relief of a world which lived for its sensations, and ignored the will--the world of Des Esseintes! Was it decadent? Yes, and thank God. Yes; here was a human being who had time to feel and experiment with his feelings, to taste and smell and arrange books and fabricate flowers, and be selfish and himself."
    Reprinted: 1946.4; 1947.1; 1953.5; 1955.8; 1962.5.

1937

1 McCOLE, C. JOHN. <u>Lucifer at Large</u>. New York: Longmans, Green, p. 223.
    Publication of <u>A Rebours</u> in America some years ago is symptomatic "of our growing fondness for that kind of morbid microscopy which has since been filtering into our fiction with an ever increasing thoroughness."

2 MOORE, GEORGE. <u>Confessions of a Young Man</u>. London: Heinemann.
    [<u>See</u> note appended to 1888.1.]

1938

1 FORD, FORD MADOX. <u>The March of Literature</u>. New York: Dial, p. 847.
    Huysmans was "a greater artist than Zola."

2 KEELER, SISTER MARY JEROME. <u>Catholic Literary France from Verlaine to the Present Time</u>. Milwaukee: Bruce, pp. 21-38.
    General discussion of Huysmans' life and works. His novels have little plot and few incidents, but they fascinate because of "their penetrating psychology, their supernatural realism, their brilliant satire, and their original though eccentric style." In 1897, he was elected first president of the Goncourt Academy. In 1905, he was nominated Chevalier of the Legion of Honor. Most important, "he inaugurated a period of real intellectual and spiritual efflorescence in France."

3 NORMAN, MRS. GEORGE. "Huysmans." <u>Dublin Review</u>, 203 (July), 51-61.
    In <u>A Rebours</u>, Huysmans reached the limit of insult to society and to himself. In a review of the book, Barbey d'Aurevilly predicted that "after writing such a book, nothing remains to M. Huysmans but to blow out his brains or to become a Christian." Huysmans, tired of depicting

1938

folly and debauchery in his fiction, tried new paths and
discovered the Church. He was lured by the strange convic-
tion that religion is not only the great vivifier but the
great narcotic, the great provider of sensations.

4   SMITH, MAXWELL. "Joris-Karl Huysmans." French Review, 11
     (February), 294-302.
          Bio-critical essay on "the most paradoxical figure in
     modern French literature." Focuses on Huysmans' early nov-
     els in their chronological order. Attempts to explain the
     apparent inconsistencies of his complex nature. Discusses
     A Rebours as "a monograph on aesthetic neurasthenia," and
     Là-Bas as "the strangest and most indefinable work of Huys-
     mans." En Route is read as "a psychological confession
     . . . of the struggle of the author . . . to throw off the
     temptations of the flesh and devote himself to a life of
     penance and prayer." La Cathédrale and L'Oblat are "hard
     reading for any but the specialist in medieval architecture
     . . . and church liturgy." Finally, Huysmans is labelled
     "one of the most overrated of French novelists"; but one
     who, nevertheless, "will always occupy his historical niche
     in the transition from the Naturalistic novel to the fin-
     de-siècle Symbolism, Decadence and Mysticism foreshadowed
     by Baudelaire and continued by Mallarmé and Verlaine in
     poetry, by Barbey d'Aurevilly, Villiers de l'Isle-Adam and
     Remy Gourmont in the novel."

1939

1   HICKS, GRANVILLE. Figures of Transition: A Study of British
     Literature at the End of the Nineteenth Century. New York:
     Macmillan, pp. 254-58.
          Moore and Wilde paid tribute to A Rebours by imitating
     it. Huysmans' novel is important, however, less because of
     its direct influence than because of "its revelation of the
     animus of decadence . . . and the personality of the deca-
     dent artist." Des Esseintes could stand, mutatis mutandis,
     for Huysmans, Baudelaire, Verlaine, and Mallarmé, as well
     as for Dowson, Symons, Johnson, Beardsley, and Wilde. One
     cannot but suspect, though, that the doctrine of art for
     art's sake was not enough in itself to support these fig-
     ures.
          Reprinted: 1969.12.

2   JACKSON, HOLBROOK. The Eighteen Nineties: A Review of Art
     and Ideas at the Close of the Nineteenth Century. Harmonds-
     worth, Middlesex: Penguin, pp. 28, 58, 61, 63, 136, 223.
          Reprint of 1913.2.

3   MOORE, GEORGE. <u>Confessions of a Young Man</u>. Harmondsworth,
      Middlesex: Penguin.
         [<u>See</u> note appended to 1881.1.]

<u>1940</u>

1   DOUGLAS, ALFRED. <u>Summing Up</u>. London: Richards, p. 105.
         <u>A Rebours</u> is "a tedious book and the least successful
      book that Huysmans ever wrote." Critics should not compare
      it with <u>Dorian Gray</u>. Wilde's novel is "as different from
      <u>A Rebours</u> as chalk from cheese."

2   ETKIN, RUTH. "The Reputation of Joris-Karl Huysmans in Eng-
      land and America." Master's thesis, Columbia University.

3   FAY, ELIOT C. "Huneker's Criticism of French Literature."
      <u>French Review</u>, 14 (December), 130-37.
         Huneker was one of the most stimulating critics of
      French literature, and his essays on Huysmans were "to some
      extent the work of a pioneer."

4   WINWAR, FRANCES. <u>Oscar Wilde and the Yellow 'Nineties</u>. New
      York: Harper, pp. 114, 155, 156-57, 158, 159, 160, 165-66.
         Discusses why Wilde accepted <u>A Rebours</u> as "the gospel of
      a fascinatingly wicked religion." One chapter of his
      <u>Dorian Gray</u> is almost a synthesis of Huysmans' novel.
      Dorian is kin to Melmoth, but Des Esseintes is "the true
      blood brother."

<u>1941</u>

1   SLOANE, JOSEPH C. "Religious Influences on the Art of Jean-
      Louis Forain." <u>Art Bulletin</u>, 23 (September), 199-206.
         In <u>L'Art moderne</u> Huysmans wrote favorably of Forain.
      The similarity in their work helps to explain why the two
      became lifelong friends. Forain, like Huysmans, also had
      a religious experience. Letters exchanged with Huysmans
      tell of Forain's spiritual orientation, in which Huysmans
      "played a considerable but probably not solitary part."
      Religious plates the artist began in 1907 were produced as
      a memorial to Huysmans.

1942

1942

1   CORNELL, WILLIAM KENNETH. <u>Adolphe Retté</u>. New Haven, Conn.: Yale Univ. Press, pp. 21, 82, 93, 101, 106, 170, 174, 177, 181, 182, 186, 193, 202, 204-206, 208, 235, 242, 244.

        After Huysmans had just published <u>La Cathédrale</u>, Retté wrote an essay to demonstrate that Huysmans' conversion was a consequence of stomach disorders, misogyny, and an unhealthy aesthetic outlook. He also composed an attack on <u>Les Foules de Lourdes</u>, ridiculing its religious sentiments. The Church, as Retté viewed it, was a relic of an outworn age; but after his own conversion in 1906, he called upon Huysmans to ask pardon for past insults. Huysmans, suffering from the cancer that was to kill him, received Retté kindly. From Huysmans, Retté came to accept "the purifying power of illness, especially since it served to bring Huysmans closer to God."

2   LITTLEFIELD, DOROTHY A. "Des Esseintes and the Aesthetic Way of Life." Master's thesis, Columbia University.

1943

1   MOORE, GEORGE. <u>Confessions of a Young Man</u>. New York: Carlton House.

        [<u>See</u> note appended to 1888.1.]

1945

1   BROWN, STEPHEN and T. McDERMOTT. <u>A Survey of Catholic Literature</u>. Milwaukee: Bruce, pp. 155, 203, 204.

        Labels Huysmans "a strange figure" who once described ugly things in ugly terms, yet his later novels are "full of wonderful descriptions of liturgy and art." With a keen sense of the absurdity of human affairs, Huysmans ridiculed without mercy--even petty and unpleasant aspects of the Church, "though his faith was deep and genuine."

2   GAUNT, WILLIAM. <u>The Aesthetic Adventure</u>. London: Jonathan Cape, pp. 114, 117-18, 143-44, 155, 167.

        Wilde discovered that many of Whistler's views on nature and art had been picked up from Baudelaire, Gautier, and "a wonderful new book that everyone was talking about, Huysmans' <u>A Rebours</u>." Flaubert and Huysmans affected Wilde profoundly with the strangeness of the beauty they sought. Had Wilde not so greatly admired <u>A Rebours</u>, "he might have pursued a safer course." At his trial, Wilde admitted that

he had been influenced by Huysmans' novel, but he refused
to be cross-examined upon the work of another artist.   To
discuss A Rebours in a court, Wilde protested, would be "an
impertinence and a vulgarity."

1946

1   BROPHY, LIAM. "Hater of Half Creeds." Grail, 28 (August),
     267-68.
         Huysmans' spiritual odyssey took him "from brothels and
     black masses to a Benedictine monastery." His books are
     milestones in his journey.

2   CONOVER, H. F. "J.-K. Huysmans: Selected References in Eng-
     lish." Washington: Library of Congress, Bibliographical
     Section.
         Three typewritten pages containing twenty-seven biblio-
     graphical listings.

3   ELLIS, HAVELOCK. Introduction to John Howard's translation of
     A Rebours. New York: Hartsdale House; Toronto: Ambassa-
     dor, pp. 11-49.
         Reprint of 1898.15.

4   FORSTER, E. M. Abinger Harvest. London: Edward Arnold,
     pp. 90, 106.
         Reprint of 1936.2.

5   SAURAT, DENNIS. Modern French Literature, 1870-1940. New
     York: Putnam's Sons, pp. 43, 50.
         Strongly negative approach to Huysmans. Though he "has
     had many admirers, probably his conversion to Catholicism
     is the real cause of his pseudo importance." Nothing that
     he wrote is of any note. "His realism is out of date, and
     his mysticism is a fake."

6   SUMMERS, MONTAGUE. "Dickens and the Decadent." Dickensian,
     42 (Spring), 61-64.
         Dickens is the only English author who satisfied Des
     Esseintes "completely and absolutely." Such a literary
     preference expressed through the protagonist of A Rebours
     is obviously Huysmans' own; yet it would be difficult to
     name any two authors more dissimilar than Huysmans and
     Dickens. The attraction of Dickens for Huysmans "lies far
     down in a psychological approach."

1946

7   [WALTON, ALAN H.]   Preface to translation of Là-Bas.   London:
    Fortune Press, pp. 5-11.
        Gives brief biographical sketch and discusses Huysmans
    as a writer "for the thoughtful man much more than for the
    person who reads for the sole purpose of passing a few
    leisure hours."   Dilates upon Là-Bas as "a masterly study
    of Satanism"; considers its structure, characterization,
    erudition.   Notes the novel is "the prelude which contains
    the leit-motif of what is to follow in En Route, La Cathé-
    drale, and L'Oblat."

1947

1   FORSTER, E. M.   Abinger Harvest.   New York: Harcourt, Brace,
    pp. 90, 106.
        Reprint of 1936.2.

2   MESPOULET, M.   "Huysmans, Joris-Karl," in Columbia Dictionary
    of Modern European Literature.   New York: Columbia Univ.
    Press, pp. 397-98.
        Bio-critical entry.   "The only true events in his life
    are those of his literary achievements, the object of his
    constant concern, and his reconversion to Catholicism in
    1892."

3   TINDALL, WILLIAM YORK.   Forces in Modern British Literature,
    1885-1946.   New York: Knopf, pp. 152, 154, 155, 161, 198,
    233, 240, 243, 270.
        Refers to Huysmans' influence on George Moore's Evelyn
    Innes and Sister Teresa, which "distinctly resemble the
    later novels of Huysmans."   Labels Là-Bas "the best account
    of Parisian occultism."   Places Huysmans in the forefront
    of the Decadent Movement.   Alludes to the importance of A
    Rebours in Wilde's writing of Dorian Gray.   Discusses
    Symons' Symbolist Movement in Literature and his essay in
    the volume devoted to Huysmans.

1948

1   ANON.   "Joris-Karl Huysmans."   Times Literary Supplement,
    no. 2402 (14 February), p. 93.
        Huysmans, unable to find anything worthy to write about,
    spent his entire life projecting his own disquietudes on to
    paper, which ultimately proved to be the most worthy sub-
    ject for his creative gifts. He used his art as though it
    were "a philosopher's stone."   His philosophy might be

termed "a search for sanction"; it makes Huysmans' work as topical as that of Huxley, Isherwood, or Green.

2   BAUGH, ALBERT C., ed. A Literary History of England. New York: Appleton-Century-Crofts, pp. 1481, 1494-95.
     The Sphinx of Wilde, which is very suggestive of the eighteen-nineties, is "suggestive of Joris-Karl Huysmans." That Moore also studied Huysmans can be shown clearly by the close parallels in A Mere Accident to A Rebours, by Evelyn Innes and Sister Teresa to Huysmans' religious novels.

3   BENET, WILLIAM ROSE. "Huysmans, Joris-Karl," in The Reader's Encyclopedia. New York: Crowell, p. 530.
     Bio-critical entry. Huysmans' style is marked by "vivid and concrete figures, fantastic description, and a gift for portraying the grotesque."

4   BROPHY, LIAM. "Route of a Realist." Irish Monthly, 76 (August), 362-67.
     Focuses on Huysmans' early naturalistic novels and the importance of A Rebours as the turning point in his life. Discussion of En Route and La Cathédrale in his evolution toward mysticism. "To follow Huysmans' itinerary is to be conscious of a fugue-like accumulation of greatness and glory realised through the keen perspective of a sensitive and scholarly mind--a mind that registered all the intellectual currents of the time."

5   BROPHY, LIAM. "Saga of Grace: Huysmans' Spiritual Evolution." Catholic World, 168 (October), 39-44.
     In honor of the centenary of his birth, this article analyzes each of Huysmans' major works in relation to the Divine pursuit of the soul.

6   HATZFELD, H. A. "Growth of French Revival." Renascence, 1 (Fall), 12-13.
     Huysmans was more than an aesthete. His privilege as a writer--after he broke with Zola and the Naturalists--was "to rediscover the beauty of the Church in her inner sanctum, her ceremonies and vestments, her architecture, music and painting, and her divine service."

7   LETTERS, FRANCIS J. H. J.-K. Huysmans: A Study. New South Wales: Westmead, 57 pp.
     Divides Huysmans' life into two periods, "the profane and the spiritual," and discusses the major works of each. Labels Marthe, Les Soeurs Vatard, and En Ménage the three

1948

outstanding products of his naturalistic period. A Rebours
is referred to as "one of the most original of books"
though "one of the most perverse." Des Esseintes is compared to Thomas Mann's Hans Castorp of The Magic Mountain.
Both are Decadents; the former retreats to Fontenay and the
latter to Davos. Castorp is seen in the more hopeless position, for though he may not have gone quite so far as
Des Esseintes, "there seems less chance of his returning
to spiritual and moral health than there is that Des Es-
seintes-Huysmans did, and this resulted in the trilogy En
Route, La Cathédrale, and L'Oblat. Of the three novels,
La Cathédrale is the most praised: "Notre Dame owes less
to Victor Hugo than Chartres to Joris-Karl Huysmans."

8   MASSIE, PATRICIA. "Arch Decadent." Southerly, 7: 180-181.
      Review of Francis J. H. Letters' J.-K. Huysmans: A
Study (see 1948.7). This study lacks balance. Too much
enthusiasm is expended in discussions of Huysmans the mystic and not enough time is given to Huysmans the critic
and historian of art, though what Letters wanted to do--
write of the "classic instance of the Decadent who becomes
a Catholic"--he does reasonably well.

9   SUMMERS, MONTAGUE. "Joris-Karl Huysmans." Time Literary Supplement, no. 2403 (21 February), p. 107.
      Letter in response to an article run 14 February 1948
(see 1948.1) states that Huysmans was not a lay brother of
the Benedictine Order but rather an oblate, the role as-
sumed following completion of the novitiate.

10 WYNDHAM-LEWIS, D. B. "A Study in Grace." Tablet [London],
192 (25 September), 200.
      Review of J.-K. Huysmans by Albert Garreau (Paris:
Tournai, 1947). The book illustrates Huysmans' themes before and after his conversion and qualifies his position as
a spiritual writer. M. Garreau has written "a lucid and
nutritious study."

1949

1   EICHMAN, MARIE M. "Joris-Karl Huysmans, Convert." Master's
thesis, St. John's University [New York].

2   HAYDEN, HIRAM and EDMUND FULLER, eds. Thesaurus of Book Di-
gests. New York: Crown, p. 16.
      Brief plot outline of A Rebours: "a classic of late
nineteenth-century 'decadent school' literature."

3   HOUGH, GRAHAM. <u>The Last Romantics</u>. London: Duckworth,
        p. 199.
            Compares <u>A Rebours</u> to Wilde's <u>Dorian Gray</u> and judges the
        former, stylistically considered, the better work.   The ex-
        traordinary vocabulary and involuted construction of Huys-
        mans are the natural expression of an odd and contorted
        sense of life, whereas "Wilde's affections are just furni-
        ture of an <u>art-nouveau</u> drawing room."   When Wilde himself
        described Huysmans' writing as "vivid and obscure at once,
        full of argot and archaicisms, of technical expressions and
        elaborate paraphrases, he put his finger on just that ele-
        ment of paradoxical vitality that his own style lacks."
        Little in <u>Dorian Gray</u> suggests that Wilde had ever really
        seen, smelt, tasted, or listened with any special percep-
        tion; <u>A Rebours</u> gives exactly the opposite impression about
        its author.

4   NICHOLSON, BENEDICT.   "Squeezing the Last Drop from Experi-
        ence: On the Writings of J.-K. Huysmans." <u>Listener</u>, 42
        (8 September), 408-409.
            Discussion of <u>L'Art moderne</u>, which though today is lit-
        tle more than "a curiosity," is still "worth reading":   it
        shows up modern art criticism as lukewarm and dishonest.
        Huysmans savagely castigated academic art and adulated a
        handful of Impressionists and realists.   He admired Degas,
        Manet, Raffaëlli, Moreau, and Rops.   Though he owned a
        sketch of Cézanne's, Huysmans was, oddly enough, less than
        enthusiastic about his work.

5   RYLAND, HOBART.   "The Marquis de Sade, Forerunner to Nine-
        teenth-Century French Literature." <u>South Atlantic Bulle-
        tin</u>, 14 (January), 9.
            De Sade was popular with nineteenth-century writers, his
        influence extending to such figures as Hugo, Flaubert,
        Barbey d'Aurevilly, and Huysmans.

6   STEEGMULLER, FRANCIS. <u>Maupassant: A Lion in the Path</u>.   New
        York: Random House, pp. 64, 98-117, 130, 137, 148-49,
        171-72.
            Maupassant, according to Huysmans, was "the life and
        soul" of Zola's circle of young admirers who met weekly at
        Médan.   Discusses their individual contributions to <u>Les
        Soirées de Médan</u>.   "Except for Huysmans, none of the other
        young contributors [Céard, Hennique, Alexis] to the <u>Soirées</u>
        was ever to display an considerable degree of creative
        originality in literature."
            Reprinted: 1972.12.

1950

1950

1   HEMMINGS, F. W. J. The Russian Novel in France, 1884-1914.
    London: Oxford Univ. Press, pp. 101-108.
        The influence of Dostoevsky, who Huysmans mentions in
    the first pages of Là-Bas, can be found in that novel; and
    "it is no far cry from Huysmans' 'spiritual naturalism' to
    Dostoevsky's 'mystical realism.'" Parallels can be found
    between passages in The Idiot and in Là-Bas; in them Dos-
    toevsky writes of Holbein's "Descent from the Cross" and
    Huysmans writes of Grunewald's "Crucifixion." But Huysmans
    never experienced more than a passing interest in the Rus-
    sian novelist. They had essentially little in common.
    Huysmans was "through and through an artist, an aesthete";
    Dostoevsky was "a metaphysician with an artist's tempera-
    ment."

2   JACKSON, HOLBROOK. The Eighteen Nineties: A Review of Art
    and Ideas at the Close of the Nineteenth Century. Har-
    mondsworth, Middlesex: Penguin, pp. 28, 58, 61, 63, 136,
    223.
        Reprint of 1912.2.

3   KEELER, SISTER JEROME. "Joris-Karl Huysmans, Benedictine
    Oblate." American Benedictine Review, 1 (March), 60-66.
        Huysmans realized after a great deal of soul-searching
    that he did not have the qualifications to become a monk,
    so instead he decided to live in the shadow of a monastery,
    keeping his liberty while profiting from the Office by be-
    coming a Benedictine oblate. He found love and joy in the
    time he spent at Ligugé, reading, writing, studying, and
    attending the Office at the abbey. In 1901, after two and
    a half years of peace and contentment, Huysmans was forced
    to return to Paris when the Benedictines were forced to
    leave Ligugé for Belgium and Spain because of anti-clerical
    laws.

4   LEHMANN, A. G. The Symbolist Aesthetic in France, 1885-1895.
    Oxford: Basil Blackwell, pp. 16, 186.
        In 1884, Mallarmé's "repute is enormously advanced by
    Huysmans' novel A Rebours."

5   REWALD, JOHN. Paul Cézanne. London: Spring Books, pp. 106,
    113, 131, 151, 152.
        As early as 1888, Huysmans was "convinced of Cézanne's
    value." He wrote of him in an article for La Cravache;
    then he devoted a whole chapter to him in Certains.

1951

1   ASHTON, DORE. "Art Books." <u>Art Digest</u>, 26 (1 October), 24.
      Review of <u>Grunewald, Le Retable D'Issenheim</u>; text by
      J.-K. Huysmans (Paris: Les Editions Braum & Cie, 1951).
      The text, written by "a principal scholar of German paint-
      ing," is an abstract from <u>Trois Eglises et Trois Primitifs</u>.
      It offers no iconographical analyses, but Huysmans' "sensi-
      tive eye selects the meaningful gestures, the occult pas-
      sages in the backgrounds and characterizations of the
      personalities in the Christ drama for a brief and literate
      commentary."

2   BUCKLEY, JEROME HAMILTON. <u>The Victorian Temper: A Study in
      Literary Culture</u>. Cambridge, Mass.: Harvard Univ. Press,
      pp. 230, 235-36.
      Des Esseintes seems "half-pathological in his misan-
      thropy and altogether morbid in his quest for exotic sensa-
      tion." Wilde restrained Dorian Gray from the complete
      Decadence of Huysmans' novel. <u>A Rebours</u>, nonetheless,
      inspired most of Wilde's lurid pages.

3   CORNELL, KENNETH. <u>The Symbolist Movement</u>. New Haven, Conn.:
      Yale Univ. Press, pp. 13, 24, 26, 30, 32, 35, 40, 43, 60,
      73, 74, 79, 82, 91, 117, 193, 197.
      In a preface dated August 1879 for the first edition of
      Theodore Hannon's <u>Rimes de joie</u>, Huysmans violently at-
      tacked the Parnassians but reserved a place of honor for
      Baudelaire. In <u>A Rebours</u>, Des Esseintes' preferences in
      modern literature are not only for the author of <u>Fleurs du
      mal</u>, but Verlaine, Corbière, and Mallarmé; and of all lit-
      erary creations, "Des Esseintes seems to me in closest har-
      mony with Mallarmé's Hérodiade." During 1887 and 1888
      Brunetière derogated those he labelled Baudelaire's imi-
      tators: "in verse, Mallarmé and Verlaine; in prose, Huys-
      mans and Poictevin." Most symbolists "appeared more inter-
      ested in Huysmans' <u>A Rebours</u> than in <u>La Cathédrale</u>, though
      the latter work is filled with the symbolism of Chartres."
      Reprinted: 1970.4.

4   H., T. B. "Bookshelf." <u>Art News</u>, 50 (October), 11.
      Review of <u>Grunewald, Le Retable d'Issenheim</u>; text by
      J.-K. Huysmans (Paris: Les Editions Braum & Cie, 1951).
      A poetic forward from <u>Trois Eglises et Trois Primitifs</u> sets
      "a satisfactorily mysterious and provoking scene."

1951

5   HATZFELD, HELMUT. "Huysmans." <u>Renascence</u>, 3 (Spring),
        187-191.
            Review-article of J. Daoust's <u>Les Débuts bénédictins de</u>
        <u>de J.-K. Huysmans</u> (Editions de Fontenelle: Abbaye Sainte-
        Wadrille) and George Veyesset's <u>Huysmans et la médicine</u>
        (Paris: Les Belles Lettres). The literary critic is not
        particularly enriched by these books. As for Dr. Veysset's
        study, the hope is expressed that "medical doctors will
        stop writing on literature as the literary historians never
        dared write on medicine."

6   NEWTON, WILLIAM. "Hardy and the Naturalists: Their Use of
        Physiology." <u>Modern Philology</u>, 49 (August), 28-41.
            Hardy was not a disciple or devotee of Zola or any of
        the French Naturalists, but he worked along their lines.
        He held to the right of the novelist to treat life frankly
        and seriously as a physiological fact, as Huysmans had
        noted in his essay "Emile Zola et L'Assommoir."

7   PRAZ, MARIO. <u>The Romantic Agony</u>. Translated by Angus David-
        son. 2nd ed. London: Oxford Univ. Press., pp. 135, 179,
        191, 296, 305-308, 310, 317, 319-26, 361, 365-67, 383, 388,
        394, 404-405, 410, 416-18, 421, 425, 427-28, 430, 448.
            Reprint of 1933.4 in a slightly revised edition.

1952

1   BALDICK, R. A. E. "Huysmans and the Goncourts." <u>French Stud-</u>
        <u>ies</u>, 6 (April), 126-34.
            Though literary historians are fond of saying that Huys-
        mans was a fervent disciple of Zola, this conception an-
        noyed Huysmans. Zola's influence was at best negligible.
        The influence of the Goncourts was far more important, as
        a study of the correspondence between Huysmans and Edmond
        de Goncourt makes clear. In a letter of March 1891, for
        example, Huysmans wrote to Edmond especially to acknowledge
        "his kinship of taste and temperament, of thought and
        style, with the Goncourts, and bore witness to their pro-
        found influence upon his work." The First President of the
        Académie Goncourt [Huysmans] "in many respects . . . ful-
        filled what the brothers had begun."

2   BROOKS, VAN WYCK. <u>The Confident Years, 1885-1915</u>. New York:
        Dutton, pp. 4, 56, 116, 151, 159, 160, 408, 562.
            Relates the interest of such American writers and crit-
        ics as Stuart Merrill, Lafcadio Hearn, Edgar Saltus, Harry
        Thurston Peck, and James G. Huneker in the life and works
        of Huysmans.

3   BROWN, ROBERT D.   "Joris-Karl Huysmans and the Bodley Head
      Decadents." Doctoral dissertation, Indian University.

4   MARTIN, ELIZABETH P.   "The Symbolist Criticism of Painting in
      France, 1880-1895 [Huysmans, Mallarmé, Verhaeren,
      LaForgue]." Doctoral dissertation, Bryn Mawr College.

5   MILLER, HENRY. The Books in My Life. New York: New Direc-
      tions, pp. 28, 317-19.
           Allusion to A Rebours. In an appendix, "The Hundred
      Books Which Influenced Me Most," Miller lists Huysmans'
      decadent novel.

6   MOORE, GEORGE. Confessions of a Young Man. London: Heine-
      mann.
           [See note appended to 1888.1.]

7   S., R. "Books Reviewed." Connoisseur [American ed.], 130
      (November), 133.
           Review of Grunewald, Le Retable d'Issenheim; text by
      J.-K. Huysmans (Paris: Les Editions Braum & Cie, 1951).
           The text is "a brilliant description with a French
      flavour, to which a summary of the painter's life is
      added."

8   WILSON, EDMUND. The Shores of Light: A Literary Chronicle of
      the Twenties and Thirties. New York: Farrar, Straus &
      Young, pp. 71, 187, 406, 697-98.
           Questions who can read Les Fleurs du Mal, A Rebours, or
      The Picture of Dorian Gray with "the enthusiasm of their
      contemporaries." Relates Swift to Huysmans: "like Huys-
      mans, he is sensitive mainly to ugly or disagreeable im-
      pressions." Swift, like Huysmans, had "an actual appetite
      for homely or sordid detail."

1953

1   ARTINIAN, ARTINE. "Huysmans to Mallarmé: An Unpublished Let-
      ter." Modern Language Notes, 67 (June), 426.
           Miscellaneous correspondence that refers to a party
      planned by Alphonse Daudet honoring the première of Renée
      Mauperin at the Odeon Theatre to which Huysmans has been
      invited. He has to decline a meeting proposed by Mallarmé
      but suggests another date.

1953

2   BALDICK, R. A. E. "Joris-Karl Huysmans." French Studies, 7
     (October), 367-69.
          Review of J.-K. Huysmans: Lettres inédites à Emile
     Zola; edited by Pierre Lambert (Genève: Droz, 1953). This
     edition of sixty letters clarifies certain aspects of Huys-
     mans' character and thought, especially in regard to his
     interpretation of Schopenhauer's philosophy and his views
     on religion at the time of writing of A Rebours. In addi-
     tion, Huysmans' criticisms of A Vau-l'Eau, A Rebours, and
     En Rade are useful to an understanding of his literary aims
     and methods. Finally, Huysmans' accounts of his relations
     with Zola's Médan group are important to students of the
     Naturalistic Movement.

3   BALDICK, R. A. E. "The Novels of Joris-Karl Huysmans." Doc-
     toral dissertation, Queens College [Oxford University].

4   EICKHORST, WILLIAM. Decadence in German Fiction. Denver:
     Allan Swallow, pp. 13-14, 15, 16, 17, 21, 39, 136.
          A type of decadent that corresponds to Huysmans' Des
     Esseintes was introduced into German literature in 1890--
     the nameless hero of Hermann Bahr's The Good School. As in
     A Rebours, "the reader is subjected . . . to a detailed,
     minute-by-minute report on the complicated reasoning that
     is supposed to go on in the mind of a modern decadent."
     Huysmans' influence is also apparent in the works of other
     German writers, especially Kurt Martens' Completion (1892)
     and his Novel of the Decadent Period (1898), as well as in
     Klaus Mann's Before Spring (1925) and his Child of Our
     Time (1932).

5   FORSTER, E. M. Abinger Harvest. London: Edward Arnold,
     pp. 90, 106.
          Reprint of 1936.2.

6   GIBSON, ROBERT. The Quest of Alain-Fournier. London: Hamish
     Miles, pp. 129, 264.
          At the end of April 1909, in an almost constant state of
     despair and remorse, conscious of his inability to live up
     to the high ideals he had set for himself, Alain-Fournier
     took to reading Les Foules de Lourdes. Though "conscious
     of its mediocrity," the book make a deep impression. He
     returned to Lourdes shortly thereafter "vaguely hoping that
     he would find there some relief for the great distress of
     his heart."

7   HEMMINGS, F. W. J. <u>Emile Zola</u>. Oxford: Clarendon Press,
        pp. 67, 90, 98, 126, 131-35, 143, 153, 164, 210, 224, 253,
        258.
              After the Franco-Prussian War, Zola had five disciples
        in Huysmans, Maupassant, Alexis, Céard, and Hennique. In
        1880, they collaborated on a volume of short stories, <u>Les</u>
        <u>Soirées de Médan</u>; Huysmans' contribution was "Sac au dos."
        In the same year there was an effort to start a newspaper
        devoted entirely to the Naturalist cause. It was to be
        called <u>La Comédie Humaine</u> and Huysmans was to edit it; but
        matters got no further than a tentative arrangement with
        printers. About the same time, however, Huysmans completed
        a pamphlet, "Emile Zola et L'Assommoir," in which he adu-
        lated Zola's novel <u>La Faute de l'Abbé Mouret</u>, calling it
        "a love-poem and one of the finest poems I know." Of the
        three Naturalists who first wrote about prostitutes, Zola's
        Nana is "an infinitely more impressive figure than Huysmans'
        Marthe or Goncourt's Elisa." In 1884, Huysmans came to feel
        that Naturalism was a cul-de-sac and he broke from Zola to
        write <u>A Rebours</u>.
              Reprinted: 1966.11 in an enlarged edition.

8   TEMPLE, RUTH ZABRISKIE. <u>The Critic's Alchemy: A Study of the</u>
        <u>Introduction of French Symbolism into England</u>. New Haven,
        Conn.: College and Univ. Press, pp. 34, 111, 123, 153,
        156, 232, 240, 251, 253-54, 284-85.
              <u>Yellow Book</u> and <u>Savoy</u> writers adopted Flaubert, Huys-
        mans, and Maupassant. Symons remarked on Huysmans' per-
        fectly decadent style and on <u>A Rebours</u> as the quintessence
        of contemporary decadence. Moore borrowed significantly
        from Huysmans, Zola, and the Goncourts.

<u>1954</u>

1   ANON. "Aesthete and Occultist." <u>London Times</u>, no. 52,885
        (20 March), p. 9.
              Review of James Laver's <u>The First Decadent</u> (<u>see</u> 1954.9).
        This biography is "the result of prolonged research," and
        it tells of Huysmans' life "with sympathy, lucidity, and
        skill."

2   ANON. "Portrait of Joris-Karl Huysmans." <u>Times Literary Sup-</u>
        <u>plement</u>, no. 2,728 (14 May), p. 316.
              Review of James Laver's <u>The First Decadent</u> (<u>see</u> 1954.9).
        This biography underlines the universal significance of
        Huysmans' earthly adventures, notwithstanding the very
        strange sidelights it gives on the different regions of

1954

human experience into which the author of A Rebours ven-
tured. Huysmans was more than the first of the Decadents:
"he was more appropriately the last of the Christians."

3   BALDICK, R. A. E. "Joris-Karl Huysmans." French Studies, 8
     (July), 279-80.
         Review of J.-K. Huysmans à la recherche de l'Unité by
     Pierre Cogney (Paris: Nizet, 1953). Strictly speaking,
     this study, which was written "with critical acumen and
     warm sympathy," is not a biography; rather it is an inves-
     tigation of Huysmans' "spiritual and intellectual develop-
     ment, based largely on an examination of his works and
     supported by quotations from his letters and notebooks."
     This work is important because it carefully and skillfully
     relates each of the disparate phases of Huysmans' experi-
     ence--Naturalism, pessimism, dandyism, occultism, satanism,
     and mysticism. All these excursions brought Huysmans
     "closer to that 'unity' for which he yearned."

4   BALDICK, R. A. E. "The First Decadent." French Studies, 8
     (October), 376-77.
         Review of James Laver's The First Decadent (see 1954.9).
     Written in an attractive style with a high regard for its
     subject, this study nevertheless contains many inaccuracies
     and major omissions. Though "a very readable work," it
     must be treated with caution.

5   BOORMAN, J. T. "A Forgotten Novelist." Manchester Guardian,
     no. 33,543 (30 April), p. 4.
         Review of James Laver's The First Decadent (see 1954.9).
     This study gives "a vivid impression of both Huysmans and
     of his work."

6   BRANDRETH, H. R. T. "The Strange Life of Joris-Karl Huys-
     mans." Theology, 57 (December), 456-61.
         Review of James Laver's The First Decadent (see 1954.9).
     Recounts Huysmans' life, which "poses universal problems."
     Attempts to account for the interest in him and his works
     nearly fifty years after his death. Concludes that this
     volume is a good introduction, for it serves "to whet the
     appetite for a more complete study." Regrets that since
     Huysmans has had so many English admirers, Laver's study
     fails to list the many translations of Huysmans' works.

7   BRERETON, GEOFFREY. A Short History of French Literature.
     London: Penguin, pp. 128, 226, 228-29, 232.
         Huysmans early in his career was "a whole-hearted adher-
     ent to Zola . . . and wrote proletarian novels in which

life was petty and sordid." Disaffected, he turned to
Impressionism and Symbolism, discovered the darker side of
Baudelaire, and wrote A Rebours, a novel that remains "a
notable wax model of the protesting aesthete attempting to
transform an abhorred materialism into a spiritualism full
of strange thrills." Huysmans continued his odyssey in
La-Bas, En Route, La Cathédrale, and L'Oblat. His books
confirm that he was "a prose stylist of great richness and
originality."
Reprinted: 1956.6; 1961.2; 1965.2; 1966.3; 1976.2.

8   BRERETON, GEOFFREY. "The Watcher from the Ceiling." New
Statesman and Nation, 47 (10 April), 478.
Review of James Laver's The First Decadent (see 1954.9).
This is "an absorbing yet scrupulous biography, not more
sensational than the subject demands and excellent as an
introduction to the writer." A Rebours should be recalled
as "the classic statement of fin-de-siècle aestheticism
. . . which Wilde imitated somewhat pallidly in Dorian
Gray."

9   LAVER, JAMES. The First Decadent: Being the Strange Life of
J.-K. Huysmans. London: Faber & Faber; New York: Cita-
del Press, 283 pp.
This first full-length biography of Huysmans in English
develops a portrait of him as the "First" Decadent. Directed more to the general reader than to the scholar, a
vividly written text presents a colorful picture of the
last years of the nineteenth century--and then tries to
fit Huysmans into that picture. Huysmans, however, was
hardly the "First" Decadent, nor was he the inventor of
"art for art's sake," nor quite the morbid man of genius
that Laver makes him out to be. The chief defects of this
study stem from the fact that its author relied too heavi-
ly on Huysmans' novels for biographical insights. Of its
fourteen chapters, the fifth, which focuses on A Rebours,
is the most informative and most interesting; it explains
the genesis of the novel, its make-up, and its importance
in Huysmans' life and the literature of the Decadence; but
it is hyperbolical to maintain that "Des Esseintes is simply Huysmans himself transported into a larger world
. . . ," that "Des Esseintes is Huysmans." Occasional
footnotes and a general bibliography enhance the value of
this study somewhat; yet it overplays Huysmans the Decadent at the expense of Huysmans the man of letters.

1954

10   M., W. P.   "Review."   <u>Dublin Magazine</u>, n.s. 30 (July-
       September), 61-63.
           Review of James Laver's <u>The First Decadent</u> (<u>see</u> 1954.9).
       Though this biography should not be missed by any who are
       interested in the development of the Decadent Movement in
       France and England, "somehow we never really come face to
       face with Huysmans."

11   STARKIE, ENID.   "The First Decadent."   <u>Blackfriars</u>, 35 (June),
       288-89.
           Review of James Laver's <u>The First Decadent</u> (<u>see</u> 1954.9).
       The value of this biography is impaired by its failure to
       include recent research and discoveries. Huysmans' por-
       trait, however, is built up with considerable literary
       skill. More than likely, this study will bring readers to
       Huysmans' novels, especially <u>A Rebours</u>, "an essential work
       for the understanding of the French Symbolist Movement."

12   STEINBERG, S. H., ed.   "Huysmans, Joris-Karl," in <u>Cassell's</u>
       <u>Encyclopedia of World Literature</u>. New York: Funk & Wag-
       nalls, p. 1056.
           Bio-critical entry. "The contrast between his spiritual
       ideals and the peculiar naturalism of his expression . . .
       his most personal and individual contribution . . . is
       best seen in <u>En Route</u> and <u>La Cathédrale</u>."

13   SULLIVAN, EDWARD D.   <u>Maupassant the Novelist</u>. Princeton,
       N.J.: Princeton Univ. Press, pp. 13, 14, 16.
           Maupassant was enthusiastic about Huysmans' <u>A Vau-l'Eau</u>
       and expressed his views in a review published in the
       March 9, 1882 issue of <u>Gaulois</u>. The "hideous truths" of
       the novel moved him profoundly.

14   TOYNBEE, P.   "Fin de Siècle."   London <u>Observer</u>, no. 8,493
       (14 March), p. 9.
           Review of James Laver's <u>The First Decadent</u> (<u>see</u> 1954.9):
       "a well-documented 'atmospheric' biography." Huysmans is
       easily the most interesting of the Decadents, but somehow
       he seems to have eluded his intelligent and scholarly
       biographer.

15   TRUDGIAN, HELEN.   "Decadence."   <u>Dublin Review</u>, 228 (Winter),
       485-86.
           Review of James Laver's <u>The First Decadent</u> (<u>see</u> 1954.9).
       Laver's powers of description and use of dramatic effect
       are in evidence. This biography, however, contains several
       inaccuracies; furthermore, there is little sympathy between
       biographer and subject and Huysmans' character suffers as
       a consequence.

16   TURNELL, MARTIN. "Romantics and Decadents." <u>Spectator</u>,
        no. 6567 (7 May), pp. 559-60.
              Review of James Laver's <u>The First Decadent</u> (<u>see</u> 1954.9):
        "an admirable biography which is a pleasure to read."
        Huysmans is a good example of a writer who imposed himself
        on a feverish, hectic, over-ripe period and changed ways of
        thinking and feeling. His <u>A Rebours</u> "broke fresh ground."
        <u>Là-Bas</u> opened "a frontal attack on Naturalism." <u>En Route</u>,
        <u>La Cathédrale</u>, and <u>L'Oblat</u> reversed the trend of writing
        about the spiritual and moral collapse of an individual:
        "they record a slow and painful ascent, the abandonment of
        the pessimism which permeated the age."

17   WALL, BERNARD. "Joris-Karl Huysmans." <u>Month</u>, 11 (June),
        363-65.
              Review of James Laver's <u>The First Decadent</u> (<u>see</u> 1954.9).
        This study is "very much of a life and times of Huysmans."
        Unfortunately, some details are not fully covered, espe-
        cially his friendship and subsequent quarrel with Léon
        Bloy.

<u>1955</u>

1   ANON. "Huysmans the Man." <u>Times Literary Supplement</u>,
        no. 2794 (15 September), p. 539.
              Review of Robert Baldick's <u>The Life of J.-K. Huysmans</u>
        (<u>see</u> 1955.3). This whole treatment of Huysmans' life is
        conventional. The biographer's emotion is mainly that of
        the thesis-writer's loyalty towards his subject; and he,
        therefore, rigidly eschews interpretation. Because of the
        determination to deal only with external facts, Huysmans
        still remains a remote and mysterious figure.

2   BALDICK, ROBERT. "Huysmans." <u>New Statesman and Nation</u>, 50
        (6 August), 163.
              Letter to the editor defending his <u>Life of J.-K. Huys-</u>
        <u>mans</u> (<u>see</u> 1955.3) against charges made by Enid Starkie (<u>see</u>
        <u>1955.19</u>) that he leaned too heavily on the autobiographical
        nature of Huysmans' novels and that his system of notes is
        faulty.

3   BALDICK, ROBERT. <u>The Life of J.-K. Huysmans</u>. Oxford: Clar-
        endon, 425 pp.
              In his will, Huysmans directed that his correspondence
        and private papers remain unpublished. Not until the death
        of his executor, Lucien Descaves, in 1949, did it become
        possible to write a reliable, fully documented biography.
        Baldick obtained access to all of Huysmans' unpublished

1955

materials. In addition, he interviewed men and women who
had known Huysmans during his last years. The result is a
detailed and authoritative account of the novelist's life.
Divided into three major parts, the text unfolds Huysmans'
life step by step. Part I is made up of eight chapters
that focus on such subjects as "The Boy," "The Student,"
"The Soldier," "The Journalist," "The Pessimist," and "The
Art Critic." Part II, also made up of eight chapters, covers such aspects of Huysmans' life as "The Decadent," "The
Occultist," "The Penitent," and so on. Part III, once
again in eight chapters, focuses on such subjects as "The
Retreatant," "The Symbolist," "The Oblat," and "The Hagiog-
rapher." Each one of the twenty-four chapters relates
Huysmans' life to his literary endeavors. An epilogue con-
cludes with an appraisal of Huysmans' importance as "one of
the most individual and yet representative writers of his
age." In trying to explain "the widespread and fervent interest in Huysmans," Baldick attributes it mainly to Huysmans' novels: "the principal merit and attraction of these
lie in their autobiographical quality; they appeal to us as
perhaps the most profound and candid memoirs produced by a
modern writer, as an intimate record of the author's material and spiritual life." Huysmans' determination to tell
the truth about himself as far as he was able, and the
psychological insight, the skill, and the honesty which he
showed in his efforts to achieve this ambition, "evoke the
admiration of present-day readers accustomed to twentieth-
century novels of introspection." Besides their interest
and importance as "human documents," Huysmans' novels have
considerable historical significance: "each of his major
works epitomizes some vital phase of the aesthetic, spiritual, or intellectual life of late nineteenth-century
France."

4   BULLOUGH, G. "A Tormented Man." Birmingtom Post (5 July),
    p. 3.
       Review of Robert Baldick's The Life of J.-K. Huysmans
    (see 1955.3): "a fully documented and well-written study
    which brings into scholarly focus the career of a tireless
    self-projector who made fiction from several stages of his
    spiritual pilgrimage." Huysmans, "a tormented man," was
    not a great writer, but he did embrace "a thousand-and-one
    complex nuances of modern humanity" in his unique and in-
    fluential books.

5   CAZAMIAN, LOUIS. A History of French Literature. Oxford:
    Clarendon Press, pp. 364-65.
       Huysmans' early novels treat of the most sordid aspects
    of life. A Rebours, however, is a work that describes a

man's desperate attempt to escape the nauseating monotony and mediocrity of fate by recourse to a general policy of artificiality. This might have some kinship with the school of Pater and the aesthetes, but Huysmans sought for spiritual values. The stages of his acceptance of Catholicism are told in En Route and La Cathédrale, which gave full scope "to the mystical and enthusiastic ritualism that was the mainstay of his faith." What keeps interest in Huysmans' books alive is "the individuality of their style. . . ." His power of conveying the sensations of both ordinary and mystical experience is "the badge of the born writer."

6   CHALKIN, MILTON. "The Influence of French Realism [Zola and Huysmans in particular] on George Moore's Early Fiction." Doctoral dissertation, New York University.

7   CONNOLLY, CYRIL. "A Romantic Realist: The Life and Works of J.-K. Huysmans." Sunday Times [London], (19 June), p. 6.
         Review of Robert Baldick's The Life of J.-K. Huysmans (see 1955.3): "bulges with a mass of new information . . . about one of the most fascinating of writers and most enigmatic of men." All Huysmans' books are autobiographical. His A Rebours is really "a bundle of essays of uneven excellence." His religious novels are "smothered in documentation." "Only Là-Bas has a real construction" and it is "one of the greatest novels I know."
         Reprinted: 1963.4.

8   FORSTER, E. M. Abinger Harvest. New York: Meridian Books, Noonday Press, pp. 90, 106.
         Reprint of 1936.2.

9   FRIEDMAN, MELVIN. Stream of Consciousness: A Study in Literary Method. New Haven, Conn.: Yale Univ. Press, pp. 37, 122, 140.
         Mallarmé and Huysmans had "a presentiment of what Joyce was later to discover." In A Rebours, Huysmans presents an extended digression in Wagnerian aesthetics. Des Esseintes tries to achieve, through contemplation, a sort of musical synthesis of various sense-impressions. Huysmans recognized "the immense possibilities of interior monologue."

10   GUTHRIE, RAMON. "Huysmans and His Time." New York Herald Tribune Book Review, 115 (4 December), 2.
         Review of James Laver's The First Decadent (see 1954.9): "a very readable biography." Among all the fin-de-siècle writers "whose aim was to create a world of depraved

1955

aesthetic mysticism . . . Huysmans is the only one whose
works are still widely read."

11   HANNAH, W. "By Strange Paths." Month, 14 (November), 306-307.
     Review of Robert Baldick's The Life of J.-K. Huysmans
     (see 1955.3). Notes that since Huysmans' death there has
     sprung up a considerable literature about him, and that
     this study is the first "full, factual, definitive and
     copiously documented biography, the fruit of painstaking
     research, which gives a dispassionately balanced picture of
     his life against the background of France at a time of
     spiritual and literary decadence."

12   HANSON, LAWRENCE and ELIZABETH HANSON. Noble Savage: The
     Life of Gaugin. New York: Random House, pp. 39, 45-46,
     157, 159.
     Huysmans disapproved strongly of Gaugin's landscapes
     which too closely resembled those of Pissarro, but the
     critic hailed Gaugin's "Study of Nude" as a masterpiece:
     "I do not hesitate to affirm that among contemporary paint-
     ers who have worked at the nude not one has so far struck
     such a relevant note of reality. . . . Up to now Rembrandt
     alone has painted the nude."

13   LANCOUR, H. "The First Decadent." Library Journal, 80
     (1 December), 2777-78.
     Review of James Laver's The First Decadent (see 1954.9):
     "skillfully written, well-documented . . . presents a com-
     pelling and sympathetic picture of a tortured, unhappy
     genius based on the autobiographical aspects of Huysmans'
     novels."

14   LUEDERS, EDWARD. Carl Van Vechten and the Twenties. Albu-
     querque, New Mexico: Univ. of New Mexico Press, pp. 20,
     56, 69-70.
     A Rebours heavily influenced Van Vechten's novel Peter
     Wiffle. Similarities between Des Esseintes and Peter Wif-
     fle can be catalogued; both seek, through strange byways,
     ultimate sensation and revelation. They differ mainly in
     the fact that "Des Esseintes desires experience for its own
     sake, while Peter wishes to utilize it in art."

15   O'FLAHERTY, K. "Life of J.-K. Huysmans." Blackfriars, 36
     (October), 404-405.
     Review of Robert Baldick's The Life of J.-K. Huysmans
     (see 1955.3). Publication of this authoritative study is
     long overdue; its presentation of hitherto unavailable ma-
     terial puts every study of Huysmans in Baldick's debt. The
     documentation is above reproach, though the volume does

suffer one serious defect: lack of "a composite portrait" of Huysmans fails to emerge. The very wealth of scholarship that has gone into this biography blurs "the intricate lines of character which emerge."

16 POWELL, ANTHONY. "Là-Bas." Punch, 229 (6 July), 24.
     Review of Robert Baldick's The Life of J.-K. Huysmans (see 1955.3). An enormous amount of research has gone into this biography. It displays Huysmans in all his many sides and reveals a great fragment of French intellectual life in the process.

17 QUENNEL, PETER. "The Life of J.-K. Huysmans." London Magazine, 2 (October), 73-76.
     Review of Robert Baldick's The Life of J.-K. Huysmans (see 1955.3). Both as a writer and as a personality Huysmans deserves to be resurrected. This study helps to do just that; it is "one of the most absorbing biographical portraits that have come my way during the last decade." Huysmans' literary gifts may have fallen short of genius, but his A Rebours remains "a minor landmark in the history of writing."

18 SHEPPARD, LANCELOT. "Life of J.-K. Huysmans." Tablet [London], 206 (1 October), 326-27.
     Review of Robert Baldick's The Life of J.-K. Huysmans (see 1955.3). This definitive biography provides the materials for a proper appraisement of Huysmans and his work.

19 STARKIE, ENID. "Bourgeois and Artist." New Statesman and Nation, 50 (23 July), 108.
     Review of Robert Baldick's The Life of J.-K. Huysmans (see 1955.3): "the authoritative biography which supersedes all previous ones . . . the soundest, fullest and most scholarly in any language." Huysmans remains an important nineteenth-century figure. His greatest qualities lie in the beauty and variety of his style. Although he may not possess the "eternal essence" of a Baudelaire or a Flaubert, his A Rebours can never be overlooked; it must be read by anyone who wants to understand the literary climate of the age.

20 THOMAS, W. E. "J.-K. Huysmans, A Rebours: A Critical Study." Master's thesis, Wales.

1955

21   TORRES-RIOSECO, A. "A Rebours and Two Sonnets of Julian del
      Casal." Hispanic Review, 23 (October), 295-97.
           A Rebours exerted a significant influence on the life
      and poetry of Julian del Casal. To write his famous son-
      nets "Salome" and "L'Apparition," which are based on
      Moreau's paintings, Casal found inspiration in the descrip-
      tions of them written by Huysmans. Both sonnets echo Huys-
      mans pictorial setting and poetic vocabulary.

22   WILSON, A. "Labour in Vain?" London Observer, no. 8562
      (7 August), p. 8.
           Review of Robert Baldick's The Life of J.-K. Huysmans
      (see 1955.3): "scholarly and detailed" but mainly "a fac-
      tual reference work for the library shelves." Huysmans'
      biographer needs to reveal the metamorphosis of his sub-
      ject's soul for the non-specialist to understand the
      writer's "spiritual journey from Naturalism through Aes-
      theticism and Diabolism to Catholicism." This Baldick
      failed to do. Huysmans' pilgrimage is detailed without
      interest or understanding.

1956

1   ARTINIAN, ARTINE. "Huysmans." Romanic Review, 47 (October),
      225-26.
           Review of J.-K. Huysmans: Lettres inédites à Edmond
      de Goncourt; edited by Pierre Lambert (Paris: Librairie
      Nizet, 1956). This book contains forty-one letters ad-
      dressed to Goncourt between 1877 and 1896. They are not a
      record of affectionate friendship, but rather the formal
      relationship of two complicated personalities who differed
      in philosophy, temperament and aesthetic theory yet main-
      tained respect for each other's literary efforts. The
      volume is important not only for the light it sheds on two
      major figures, but also because it furnishes valuable in-
      formation on numerous other minor figures and personalities
      of the late nineteenth century.

2   ARTINIAN, ARTINE. "The Life of J.-K. Huysmans." Romanic Re-
      view, 47 (April), 153-54.
           Review of Robert Baldick's The Life of J.-K. Huysmans
      (see 1955.3): "the first fully documented biography in any
      language." No previous biographer of Huysmans enjoyed ac-
      cess to the materials assiduously compiled by M. Pierre
      Lambert of the Société Huysmans and made available to Bal-
      dick. This definitive work even supplies all available
      dates; on occasion, detailed indication of the hour of day
      of a particular incident is also given. All Huysmans'

activities, however trivial, are recorded. This biography
has all the ingredients which contribute to better interpretations and a fuller comprehension of Huysmans' literary
works.

3   BART, B. "Clarity and Irony." Renascence, 9 (Autumn), 54-56.
        Review of Robert Baldick's The Life of J.-K. Huysmans
    (see 1955.3): "a work of enduring quality and signifi-
    cance." Huysmans' conversion is the central event in this
    biography; his research into occultism is viewed as a pre-
    liminary step. The concluding pages provide a full criti-
    cal examination of Huysmans' works.

4   BEAUMONT, ERNEST. "Reviews." Modern Language Review, 51
        (January), 121-22.
        Review of Pierre Cogney's J.-K. Huysmans à la recherche
    de l'Unité (Paris: Nizet, 1953). To those interested in
    Huysmans because of his religious orientation, this book
    will prove a disappointment. The ideas which he came to
    have in his later life, though they are mentioned, are not
    treated at a level which would satisfy those concerned with
    the mystical aspects of religion.

5   BEAUMONT, ERNEST. "Reviews." Modern Language Review, 51
        (July), 440-41.
        Review of Robert Baldick's The Life of J.-K. Huysmans
    (see 1955.3): "a full-scale biography based on a thorough
    knowledge of both published and unpublished material." Of
    the various individuals with whom Huysmans came in contact,
    dubious occultists, artistic monks, pursuing women, and the
    like, sufficiently is written for the reader to gain a
    clear idea of the mileius in which the writer moved; the
    background is substantial.

6   BRERETON, GEOFFREY. A Short History of French Literature.
        London: Penguin, pp. 128, 226, 228-29, 232.
        Reprint of 1954.7.

7   BROPHY, LIAM. "Joris-Karl Huysmans, Aesthete turned Ascetic."
        Irish Ecclesiastical Record, 86 (July), 43-51.
        In trying to explain the various steps that Huysmans
    took during his life, he is often misunderstood and mis-
    represented. When he was a Naturalist, litterateurs knew
    his every thought. After En Route, which he wrote "from
    the perspective of the fresh-won heights of the supernat-
    ural, critics found his sayings hard and followed him no
    more."

1956

8   BROWN, R. D. "Suetonius, Symonds, and Gibbon in The Picture
    of Dorian Gray." Modern Language Notes, 71 (April), 264.
        A comparison of A Rebours with Dorian Gray reveals that
    since Wilde's description of A Rebours in Dorian Gray
    matches nothing found in Huysmans' novel, the sources of
    Wilde's descriptions must lie elsewhere. Suetonius' De
    vita Caesarum, Symonds' Age of Despots, and Gibbon's
    Decline and Fall of the Roman Empire are sources Wilde
    borrowed from to explain the potency of the corrupting book
    Dorian reads.

9   DOOLEY, ROGER. "The First Decadent." Catholic World, 182
    (February), 396-97.
        Review of James Laver's The First Decadent (see 1954.9).
    Commends the study for its richly detailed picture not only
    of the subject but also of the prevalent intellectual, ar-
    tistic, and religious currents of the time. If some read-
    ers still may find it difficult "to sympathize with Huys-
    mans," the fault does not lie in this presentation.

10 MAGILL, FRANK N., ed. Masterpieces of World Literature in
    Digest Form. 2nd series. New York: Harper, pp. 4-5.
        Plot summary of Against the Grain.

11 ROULEAU, SISTER M. CELESTE. "The Place of the Blessed Virgin
    Mary in the Work of Joris-Karl Huysmans." Master's thesis,
    Catholic University.

12 YAMPOLSKY, BORIS. "The First Decadent." Jubilee, 3 (Janu-
    ary), 49.
        Review of James Laver's The First Decadent (see 1954.9).
    "Despite some needless and almost boring into secondary
    characters and issue in general," this biography is still
    entertaining and informative: "a necessary book for the
    understanding of Huysmans' rather lurid works."

1957

1   CEVASCO, G. A. "After Fifty Years: Huysmans in Retrospect."
    Benedictine Review, 12 (July), 52-55.
        Review-article based on James Laver's The First Deca-
    dent (see 1954.9) and Robert Baldick's The Life of J.-K.
    Huysmans (see 1955.3). Both biographies recommend that
    "Huysmans' better books should be picked up, dusted off and
    read through." Laver's treatment is colorful but he often
    distorts his subject. Baldick's study is scholarly and
    perceptive, "the first fully documented biography of Huys-
    mans in any language." Laver emphasizes Huysmans' eccen-

tricities; Baldick focuses primarily on Huysmans the serious writer. A Rebours, as Baldick reads it, "first cracked the wall of materialism that Huysmans had built around himself." En Route he equates "to the purgative life, La Cathédrale to the illuminative life, and L'Oblat to the unitive life."

2 CEVASCO, G. A. "From the Files." Renascence, 10 (Winter), 104-105.
    Review of J.-K. Huysmans: Lettres inédites à Edmond de Goncourt; edited by Pierre Lambert (Paris: Librairie Nizet, 1956). More valuable than what the forty letters themselves contain are the annotations of their editor, Pierre Lambert. Of special interest is material related to Huysmans' becoming the first president of the Goncourt Academy.

3 CEVASCO, G. A. "Huysmans Fifty Years After." Renascence, 9 (Spring), 115-19.
    Just as any object may appear distorted and strange when viewed from a distance, so too Huysmans today often seems most erratic and insincere to those who know him least. To know him and his books is not to admire him or appreciate his literary endeavors, necessarily, but it does make for more intelligent criticism than his reputation frequently receives. What his reputation may be fifty years from now is impossible to ascertain; yet each succeeding decade of this past half-century has seen the appearance of an increasing number of books, theses, and articles devoted to his life and work.

4 HIGHET, GILBERT. "The Decadent," in his Talents and Geniuses. New York: Oxford, pp. 92-99.
    Huysmans' novels, which deal with the problem of suffering, the mystery of evil, and the consciousness of sin, have had a strong but limited influence. The great merits of his work are his extraordinarily vivid style, with its complex and varied sentence structure, and his uncanny power to evoke physical feelings, particularly those associated with revulsion and pain. His entire life revolved around two central ideas: it is possible and desirable for the human spirit to pay the same attention to ugliness that it does to beauty; and, a truly sensitive soul can be as happy in suffering as in enjoying perfect physical bliss. Interestingly enough, Huysmans' books correspond closely to the novels of William Faulkner; but Faulkner "cannot or will not say clearly all that is in his tormented mind, while one of the chief merits of Huysmans' novels is

1957

that . . . he is as precise, as accurate, and as consciously clear as the Dutch artists who were his ancestors."

5   MALLARMÉ, STÉPHANE. Selected Poems. Translated by C. F.
    MacIntyre. Berkeley: Univ. of California Press,
    pp. 132-37.
        Contains "Prose pour Des Esseintes," which the poet
    wrote in tribute to Huysmans. Though the work is "consid-
    ered to be the essence of unintelligibility," a stanza-by-
    stanza explication is given of the work, relating it to A
    Rebours.

6   POMERLEAU, SISTER MARY. "Huysmans' Concept of the Liturgy."
    Benedictine Review, 12 (Winter), 56-60.
        Huysmans conceived the liturgy as inseparable from its
    artistic setting. As a result of his spiritual experiences
    during his pilgrimages to Chartres, he hoped for a renewal
    of the liturgical arts and the realization of that perfect
    ensemble the Middle Ages had created.

7   THOMAS, W. E. "J.-K. Huysmans and A Rebours." Modern Lan-
    guages, 38 (June), 56-60.
        Discusses A Rebours, "a study in abnormal psychology,"
    as the keystone in Huysmans' work. Focuses on its struc-
    ture and the character of Des Esseintes, whose "protest
    against life is seen in his literary and aesthetic predi-
    lections." Dilates upon the "international significance"
    of A Rebours, for it has become "an important landmark in
    the history of the modern novel."

1958

1   ANON. "The Devil's Disciple." Time, 72 (21 July), 82.
        Review of Keene Wallis' translation of Là-Bas. Summa-
    rizes the narrative. Notes the novel has always "enjoyed
    a kind of scandalous celebrity among men of letters,"
    though Huysmans' own life was even more interesting than
    this book. The personal experiences that went into Là-Bas
    led Huysmans to religion, for he came to understand "that
    it is madness to believe in the Devil without believing in
    God."

2   ARTINIAN, ARTINE. "Reviews." Romanic Review, 49 (April),
    152-53.
        Review of J.-K. Huysmans, Lettres inédites à Camille
    Lemonnier; edited by G. Vanwelkenhuzen (Genève: Droz,
    1957). These letters reflect the affectionate friendship
    which characterized their relationship. They are familiar,

chatty epistles, sparking with the colorful language Huysmans often employed. Prepared by an outstanding historian
of Franco-Belgic literary relations, this volume serves
Huysmansian scholarship admirably.

3   BALDICK, ROBERT. Introduction to Keene Wallis' translation of
    Là-Bas. Evanston, Illinois and New York: University
    Books, pp. vii-xxviii.
        Discussion of the genesis of the novel, the research
    that went into it, and the curious individuals Huysmans
    actually met who appear as its leading characters. Briefly
    covers its critical reception: "the public acclaimed it"
    and it brought Huysmans both "faith and fame." The enor-
    mous mass of occult information in the volume "may be re-
    garded as a trustworthy picture of the occultist scene in
    late nineteenth-century France."

4   BRAUN, SIDNEY D. "Huysmans, Joris-Karl," in Dictionary of
    French Literature. New York: Philosophical Library,
    pp. 158-59.
        Bio-critical entry. "Although in his documentation,
    Huysmans is naturalistic, his pre-occupation with literary
    form relates him more openly to Flaubert and the Goncourt
    brothers."
        Reprinted: 1965.1.

5   CARTER, A. E. The Idea of Decadence in French Literature.
    Toronto: Univ. of Toronto Press, pp. 17, 18-20, 80-86,
    89-94, 132-34, 135-36, 151.
        Les Soeurs Vatard and A Rebours are "in many ways cen-
    tral points in the evolution of decadent sensibility: a
    perfect equilibrium between the aesthetic decadence of
    Gautier and Baudelaire and the naturalistic decadence of
    Zola and Céard." Huysmans' preference for the modern to
    the ancient, and his habit of identifying both with arti-
    ficiality and decadence, came from Gautier and Baudelaire;
    from Zola he learned to interpret decadence in psychologi-
    cal terms. An analysis of the makeup of Des Esseintes is
    used to support such a contention. "A Rebours . . . con-
    tains a full discussion of the decadent style," but it may
    be questioned if Huysmans, as he traced out the manias of
    Des Esseintes, realized fully what he was doing.

6   CEVASCO, G. A. "J.-K. Huysmans and the Impressionists."
    Journal of Aesthetics and Art Criticism, 17 (December),
    201-207.
        Describes the stages of Huysmans' career as an art crit-
    ic. The Impressionists regarded him as one of their most
    able defenders and as a pioneer of an Impressionist

1958

movement in literature. In his reviews he avoided the "in-
nocuous jargon" favored by most critics of the time. From
Huysmans alone descends almost all the valid criticism of
Impressionism; and, significantly, most of his judgments
have become universally acceptable.

7   CUSHING, H. "Down There." Catholic Library World, 30
        (October), 41.
            Review of Keene Wallis' translation of Là-Bas. In one
        respect, the materials of this novel are obscene, since
        not only are the practices of the notorious Gilles de Rais
        recounted at great length, but paralleling them are pre-
        sented the orgies, particularly the blasphemous black mass
        of nineteenth-century satanists. The work, however, is
        more than a study of the obscene and the diabolical: it is
        rather a presentment of Huysmans' deepening dissatisfaction
        with both philosophic and literary naturalism and his
        heightened awareness of spiritual dimensions.

8   MAGILL, FRANK N. "Huysmans, Joris-Karl," in Cyclopedia of
        World Authors. New York: Harper & Row, pp. 545-46.
            Bio-critical entry. Lists principal writings and dis-
        cusses A Rebours and Là-Bas. "Aside from his influence on
        the literature of the 1890's, Huysmans has a genuine impor-
        tance in that he so well depicted a characteristic problem
        of the late nineteenth century: the struggle to regain the
        religious faith . . . which had been lost by so many." In
        his fiction neither sensual indulgence nor the enjoyment of
        art could fill the spiritual vacuum in the lives of his
        chief characters.

9   SYMONS, ARTHUR. "The Later Huysmans," in his The Symbolist
        Movement in Literature. New York: Dutton, pp. 75-84.
            Reprint of Part II of 1919.7.

1959

1   BALDICK, ROBERT. Introduction to his translation of A Rebours.
        London and Baltimore, Md.: Penguin, pp. 5-14.
            Relates Huysmans' early background and how he came to
        write the novel: "This book was originally conceived as an
        esoteric extension of A Vau-l'Eau." Focuses on the charac-
        ter of Des Esseintes, who owes something "to half-a-dozen
        dandies and aesthetes who were living or only lately dead
        when Huysmans wrote A Rebours." Discusses the makeup of
        the novel and dilates upon several chapters. Accounts for
        the immediate popularity of the work, which "fell like a
        meteorite into the literary fairground, provoking anger and

stupefaction, especially among the press." As for the influence of A Rebours, "the total number of Des Esseintes'
literary progeny is incalculable: almost every unhappy,
solitary hero of a twentieth-century novel could probably
trace his descent back to Huysmans' great creation." The
significance of the work transcends literary history; for
Des Esseintes is, "above all else, the modern man par ex-
cellence, tortured by that vague longing for an elusive
ideal . . .; torn between desire and satiety, hope and disillusionment; painfully conscious that his pleasures are
finite, his needs infinite."

2 FIXLER, M. "Affinities between J.-K. Huysmans and the Rosi-
   crusian Stories of W. B. Yeats." PMLA, 74 (September),
   464-69.
      Huysmans was something of a Manichean; he sought experi-
   mental evidence to confirm the existence of opposing forces
   of good and evil, and when he had the evidence he sought
   for he rejected the Devil. The inversion of values in A
   Rebours and of ritual in Là-Bas failed to reconcile the opposition between good and evil, between false and true worship, as Yeats tried to do in his Rosicrucian stories of
   1896. Yeats' "The Adoration of the Magi," "The Tables of
   the Law," and "Rosa Alchemica" owe something to A Rebours,
   for the protagonists of all three stories are recluses like
   Des Esseintes. In "Rosa Alchemica," furthermore, the decor
   of the narrator's house recalls Des Esseintes' refuge at
   Fontenay. Yeats had certainly read Huysmans and the works
   of professional occultists.

3 HARVEY, SIR PAUL and J. E. HESELTINE, eds. "Huysmans, Joris-
   Karl," in The Oxford Companion to French Literature. Oxford: Clarendon Press, p. 353.
      Bio-critical entry. Huysmans' novels and critical es-
   says were written in "an elaborate, mannered style, full of
   neologisms and syntactical contortions."

4 JOYCE, JAMES. "A French Religious Novel," in Critical Writings of James Joyce. Edited by Ellsworth Mason and Richard
   Ellman. New York: Viking, p. 123.
      Antipathetic toward Catholicism and disappointed with La
   Cathédrale, Joyce complained that as a novelist Huysmans
   was becoming "more formless and . . . obviously comedian."

1959

5   KOCH-EMMERY, E. "Against Nature, A New Translation of A Re-
     bours." AUMLA [Journal of the Australasian Universities
     Language and Literature Association], no. 11 (September),
     pp. 102-104.
         Review of Robert Baldick's translation of A Rebours:
     "perfect in the sense it does not read like a translation."
     Nothing essential has been altered; in fact, Baldick tends
     only to embellish a great deal. He has done a good job
     translating from one language to another and from one cen-
     tury to the next. His style is rhythmical, readable, and
     does full justice to the original text.

6   MOORE, GEORGE. Confessions of a Young Man. New York: Capri-
     corn Books, G. P. Putnam's Sons.
         [See note appended to 1888.1.]

7   PRITCHARD, V. S. "Silk Socks in the Bookcase." New States-
     man, 57 (21 March), 412.
         Review of Robert Baldick's translation of A Rebours.
     Huysmans' novel is always worth republishing; it is "a fas-
     cinating allegory of the brief pleasure and fetal agonies
     of escapism." This translation catches "the alacrity of
     the author's intelligence and its modish touch." Baldick
     is right when he states in an Introduction that A Rebours
     has not become musty, that it has "a good deal of moral
     survival left in it."

8   SENIOR, JOHN. "Between the Bullet and the Church," in his The
     Way Down and Out: The Occult in Symbolist Literature.
     Cornell: Cornell Univ. Press, pp. 117-44.
         Des Esseintes represents a parody and at the same time a
     paradigm of literary occultism. A Rebours is a meticulous
     documentation of the life of its author as he would have
     wished to have led it, though he remained oddly detached
     from the dream. In Là-Bas, Huysmans sought more direct oc-
     cult experience; for this novel was "the very center of a
     serious spiritual crisis, and a general crisis in the his-
     tory of modern literature." Despite Huysmans' conversion
     to Catholicism, his work suggests that he maintained "an
     occult sensibility."

9   TURNELL, MARTIN. The Art of French Fiction. New York: New
     Directions, pp. 16, 24-25, 28, 312, 313.
         Some of the most influential writers of the nineteenth
     century "were men like the Goncourts and Huysmans who can-
     not be regarded as novelists of the first order." They
     made an extraordinary impact upon style, though they over-
     worked their devices. Huysmans' practice of separating

words from their syntactical group can be seen as "one form of the nineteenth-century attack upon grammar."

10   VAN GOGH, VINCENT. Complete Letters. Vol. III. Greenwich, Conn. and New York: Graphic Society, 426, 458, 492.
      In a letter from Paris written during the summer or autumn of 1887 to his sister Wilhelmina, Van Gogh adulates the French Naturalists, Zola, Maupassant, and Huysmans. Again from St. Remy at the end of September 1889, he expresses his "boundless admiration" for certain French writers, Huysmans among them. From Arles in June 1888, he wrote of Huysmans' En Ménage and quoted the artist character Cyprien: "The most beautiful pictures are those one dreams about when smoking pipes in bed, but which one will never paint."

11   WEIGHTMAN, J. G. "Perfumes and Perversions." London Observer, no. 8750 (15 March), p. 22.
      Review of Robert Baldick's translation of A Rebours: "an excellent new translation." This novel once "flared through the literary heavens like a great rocket . . . all that is left today is a charred and empty case."

12   WILSON, EDMUND. Axel's Castle: A Study in the Imaginative Literature of 1870-1930. New York: Scribner, pp. 10, 18, 48, 49, 94, 264-65, 267.
      Reprint of 1931.12.

1960

1   CEVASCO, G. A. "On Huysmans." Critic, 19 (December), 8.
      A letter to the editor critical of Lancelot C. Sheppard's "Joris-Karl Huysmans: From Naturalism to Catholicism" (see 1960.6). Explains, among other things, why Robert Baldick, an Englishman, was the first to produce the definitive life of Huysmans (see 1955.3) instead of one of Huysmans' "faithful band of admirers" in France.

2   FRANKL, PAUL. The Gothic: Literary Sources and Interpretations through Eight Centuries. Princeton, N.J.: Princeton Univ. Press, pp. 275, 660-63.
      La Cathédrale is Huysmans' "great paean of praise to Chartres Cathedral." The whole book is "a revitalization of medieval symbolism . . . of allegory." In a sense, Huysmans' novel is a successor both to Chateaubriand's Genius of Christianity and Hugo's Notre Dame, though "more scholarly than the former and less novelistic than the latter." What Huysmans sought was not the body of Chartres, but its soul.

1960

3   MAGILL, FRANK N. Masterpieces of World Literature in Digest
    Form. 3rd series. New York: Harper, pp. 300-301.
        Plot summary of Là-Bas.

4   PETERS, ROBERT L. "The Salomé of Arthur Symons and Aubrey
    Beardsley." Criticism, 2 (Winter), 150-63.
        Symons' "Studies in Strange Sins" derives in varying
    degrees from his response to Beardsley's graphic art, the
    paintings of Moreau, the dramas of Wilde, and the novels of
    Huysmans.

5   PRIESTLY, J. B. Literature and Western Man. New York:
    Harper & Row, pp. 258, 259.
        In his early novels, Huysmans described life "with
    great bitterness." Later, in A Rebours he wrote "with
    considerable resources of invention and fine language, but
    not without silliness, of an existence of complete arti-
    ficiality."

6   SHEPPARD, LANCELOT C. "Joris-Karl Huysmans: From Naturalism
    to Catholicism." Critic, 19 (August), 14-15, 64-65.
        The sordidness of Huysmans' early novels reflects his
    whole-hearted allegiance to the Naturalistic Movement.
    With A Rebours he broke with Zola and developed along his
    own lines. The Naturalism of his earlier novels can be
    discerned in Là-Bas, where it degenerated into Satanism,
    but it is the turning point in Huysmans' pilgrimage. En
    Route recounts Huysmans' actual conversion, and it is
    probably his finest novel.

7   SHEPPARD, LANCELOT C. "On Huysmans." Critic, 19 (December),
    8.
        Response to a letter by G. A. Cevasco (see 1960.1).
    Maintains that Huysmans is a novelist of "second rank . . .
    but to reach the second class is no mean achievement." If
    his novels fall short, he is, nonetheless, "of absorbing
    human interest," and it is "clear that Huysmans' interest
    for us lies in the human element in his work."

8   STARKIE, ENID. From Gautier to Eliot: The Influence of
    France on English Letters, 1851-1939. London: Hutchin-
    son, pp. 82-85.
        Stresses the influence that Huysmans' concept of deca-
    dence had in England in the 1890s. Focuses on the charac-
    ter of Des Esseintes and his artificial manner of living at
    Fontenay, especially his orgue à bouche and the theory of
    correspondences. More than any other work, A Rebours

"helped to crystallize the conception of the Aesthete and
the Decadent."
Reprinted: 1971.19.

9   TINSLEY, SISTER LUCY.   "The Naturalistic Spirituality of
Joris-Karl Huysmans." PMLA, 75 (September), 424-31.
Huysmans broke with the ideas of the Naturalists when he
wrote A Rebours, but he did not abandon the extreme realism
of their style. His later style, as manifest especially in
En Route and La Cathédrale, is "a naturalistic symbolism of
spirituality."

10 ZAGONA, HELEN GRACE.   The Legend of Salomé and the Principle
of Art for Art's Sake. Genève: Librairie E. Droz; Paris:
Librairie Minard, pp. 96-102.
In A Rebours, the heroine of Moreau's "Salomé" and
"L'Apparition" is given a place of special honor and importance. An understanding of these two paintings and
Des Esseintes' reactions to them helps to clarify his
strange, deviate nature. Of all paintings, he considered
these most suitable to his visual needs: "he could spend
long nights contemplating the intriguing portraits, lost
in a dream-world where beauty, ardour and cruelty reigned."
Additionally, one of Des Esseintes' most precious books is
a volume of Mallarmé's poetry containing among its selections a fragment of "Hérodiade."

1961

1   AHNEBRINK, LARS.   The Beginnings of Naturalism in American
Fiction, 1891-1903. New York: Russell & Russell, pp. 21,
39, 309-14.
Discusses the probable influence of Huysmans on Frank
Norris, whose characters Vandover and Corthell are, "to
some extent, reminiscent of Des Esseintes," though neither
went to "the excesses and eccentricities typical of Huysmans' hero."

2   BRERETON, GEOFFREY.   A Short History of French Literature.
London: Penguin, pp. 128, 226, 228-29, 232.
Reprint of 1954.7.

3   McCARTHY, ELIZABETH.   "Character Portrayal in the Trilogy of
Joris-Karl Huysmans' En Route, La Cathédrale, L'Oblat."
Master's thesis, Catholic University.

1961

4 MACY, JOHN. The Story of the World's Literature. Revised
edition. New York: Liveright, pp. 418-19.
Huysmans has not been adequately translated into English: "his colored style is difficult to render." A
delight to the literary, "he is distinctly an author's author . . . but he is sure to become better known in the
future. . . ."

5 MASON, H. "Huysmans." Catholic Worker, 27 (March), 5-6.
Unfortunately, Huysmans is too often thought of mainly
in the context of his naturalism, eroticism, and the cult
of art-for-art's sake. Too little is known about his conversion, his days as a Benedictine oblate, and his mystical
writings. Especially valuable is his Sainte Lydwine de
Schiedam, a biography of a rather obscure fifteenth-century
saint of reparation.

6 MOORE, GEORGE. Confessions of a Young Man. London: Brown,
Watson.
[See note appended to 1888.1.]

7 PHILIPS, E. M. "Reviews." French Studies, 15 (July), 285.
Review of five books, one of which is Against Nature,
Robert Baldick's translation of A Rebours. Granted the extreme difficulty of rendering Huysmans into English "this
translation has considerable merit." Baldick has done a
good job in simplifying "Huysmans' murkily sensuous prose."

8 REWALD, JOHN. The History of Impressionism. New York:
Museum of Modern Art, pp. 404, 426, 428, 441, 447, 450,
472-75, 484, 489, 500-501, 526, 548, 553.
Covers Huysmans' debut as an art critic: "charged into
the ranks . . . with an outspokenness, a devasting irony,
and beautifully directed aim." He early commended Manet,
Degas, Forain, Raffaëlli. L'Art moderne contains his likes
and dislikes of the work of various young artists.

9 RIDGE, GEORGE ROSS. "The Decadent: A Metaphysical Hero," in
his The Hero in French Decadent Literature. Athens,
Georgia: Univ. of Georgia Press, pp. 48-66.
Analyzes the decadent aspects of Huysmans' work, which
represents "a clear reversal of classical values." A Rebours is the central work of decadent literature, and its
hero, Des Esseintes, "towers above all other heroes of the
decadence." As an archetypal aesthete, Des Esseintes iden-
tifies art with life, but art exacts a fearful toil. So,
too, does his androgynism, as played out in his relation-
ship with Miss Urania, an American acrobat. In Là-Bas,

Huysmans treats of nymphomania and la femme fatale in the character of Mme. Chantelouve. The decadent hero is impassive in his cerebral existence, a victim of his inertia. His carnal women live; he languishes.

10   SHRODER, MAURICE Z. Icarus: The Image of the Artist in French Romanticism. Cambridge, Mass.: Harvard Univ. Press, pp. 234-37, 247.
          Wilde placed Dorian Gray in "the French tradition" when his character decides to make of his life a work of art. In doing so, Wilde's model was "the yellow-backed novel in which Dorian discovered the theory of the New Hedonism, Huysmans' A Rebours. Des Esseintes is the epitome of the Decadence; in him, Huysmans "portrayed the sickly Icarus carried to the limit of his development—or more appropriately, of his degeneration." Des Esseintes' palace of art, however, proves to be "an unsatisfactory alternative to the world of common experience."

11   WILSON, EDMUND. Axel's Castle: A Study in the Imaginative Literature of 1870-1931. London and Glascow: Collins, pp. 10, 18, 48, 49, 94, 264-65, 267.
          Reprint of 1931.12.

1962

1   CEVASCO, G. A. J.-K. Huysmans in England and America: A Bibliographical Study. Charlottesville, Virginia: Bibliographical Society of the Univ. of Virginia, 30 pp.
          An unannotated checklist of books and articles in English devoted to the life and works of Huysmans. Contains a brief introduction and a selected list of translations.

2   CEVASCO, G. A. "Reviews." Books Abroad, 36 (Summer), 290.
          Review of M. Lobet's J.-K. Huysmans ou le témoin écorché (Paris: Vitte, 1960). Attempts to account for the genesis of some of Huysmans' ideas, especially his pessimism, his misogyny, his mysticism, and his interest in religious art. The explorations are worth-while; the findings, provocative.

3   CRAIG, ALEC. The Banned Books of England and Other Countries: A Study of the Conception of Literary Obscenity. London: Allen & Unwin, pp. 58, 93, 183-84.
          Là-Bas was one of four French novels in translation condemned by a British Court of Law in 1934. [The other three were works by Pierre Louys.] The novels were ob-

1962

tained through a police raid on the Fortune Press, a small
London publishing house that specialized in the work of
promising young authors and the issue of older books, gen-
erally translations, though the firm did publish some
erotica.
Reprinted: 1977.4.

4   DRINKWATER, JOHN. The Outlien of Literature. London:
Newnes, pp. 603, 607-608.
Huysmans' early work was Zolaesque in its minute, uncompromising, and relentless realism. A Rebours is an
elaborately morbid study of a decadent aristocrat. Huysmans' masterpiece is En Route, in which he describes the
conversion to mysticism of a hero modelled on himself.

5   FORSTER, E. M. Abinger Harvest. London: Edward Arnold,
pp. 90, 106.
Reprint of 1936.2.

6   GONCOURT, EDMOND and JULES DE. Pages from the Goncourt Journal. Translated and edited by Robert Baldick. London and
New York: Oxford Univ. Press, pp. 224, 231, 272, 274, 284,
294, 313, 314, 315, 333, 337, 352, 353, 362, 363-64,
371-72.
Records various meetings with Huysmans between 1876 and
1892. In an entry dated May 16, 1884, A Rebours is adulated: "The hero is a wonderful neurotic. They may say
what they like against the book, it brings a little fever
to the brain, and books that do that are the work of men
of talent. And it is written in an artistic style to
boot. . . ."

7   GRIFFITHS, RICHARD. Introduction to his translation of Croquis parisiens. London: Fortune Press, pp. 7-16.
Relates the history of the book and Huysmans' aims in
writing it: "I should like to create little sonnets,
small ballads, tiny poems, without the jingle of rhyme,
but in language as singing as verse." Refers to critiques
of early reviewers who concerned themselves more with "the
shocking aspects of certain passages and neglected the
powerful beauty of the greater part of the book." Describes Huysmans' style and discusses the difficulties of
transposing it into English.

8   JOSEPHSON, MATTHEW. Life Among the Surrealists: A Memoir.
New York: Holt, Rinehart & Winston, pp. 32, 101, 343, 345.
Comments on his early reading of A Rebours; judged
Huysmans one of "the great models of French literature."

Refers to his meeting with Léon Deffoux, who in earlier
years had been Huysmans' secretary. Deffoux disliked Zola
and the Dreyfusards; told of indiscretions in Zola's life
and showed "unpublished papers of Huysmans filled with unpleasant and intolerant reflections on Zola's moral
character."

9   HART-DAVIS, RUPERT, ed. The Letters of Oscar Wilde. London:
    Rupert Hart-Davis; New York: Harcourt, Brace & World,
    pp. 313, 352, 406, 423, 520-21, 522, 590.
        In a letter dated April 15, 1892, Wilde states that his
    Dorian Gray "is partly suggested by Huysmans' A Rebours";
    yet in a letter dated February 12, 1894, in response to a
    question about the book "that poisoned or made perfect
    Dorian Gray," Wilde claimed that there was no such book:
    "it is a fancy of mine merely." On April 6, 1897, he ex-
    pressed disappointment with En Route: "most over-rated
    . . . sheer journalism . . . never makes one hear a note of
    music it describes. The subject is delightful, but the
    style is . . . worthless, slipshod, flaccid." The titles
    of the mystical books referred to in En Route Wilde found
    "fascinating."

10 MADSEN, BORGE GEDSO. Strindberg's Naturalistic Theatre: Its
    Relation to French Naturalism. New York: Russell & Rus-
    sell, pp. 12, 16, 138, 154, 166, 172.
        As his letters indicate, Strindberg read widely in
    French naturalistic literature and was acquainted with the
    works of Huysmans. In all likelihood, Huysmans' Marthe has
    some influence on Strindberg's Mother Love.

1963

1   ADAM, ANTOINE. The Art of Paul Verlaine. New York: New York
    Univ. Press, pp. 51, 118, 120.
        In A Rebours, Huysmans praised the originality of Ver-
    laine's verse. When Verlaine's life was at its lowest ebb
    in 1887, Huysmans visited with the poet to dispel his de-
    spair and inclination toward self-destruction.

2   BRANDRETH, H. R. T. Huysmans. London: Bowes & Bowes; New
    York: Hillary House, 127 pp.
        Nine chapters treat of Huysmans' work in chronological
    sequence because "it was chronologically through his work
    that he revealed the drama of his soul." The real great-
    ness of Huysmans "lies less in his influence on French art
    and letters, considerable though these were, than in his

1963

capacity for laying himself alongside the reader who takes
the trouble to understand him, and to whom he becomes a
familiar companion." As an author, Huysmans' importance is
in "the inner struggle" which he was able to record minute-
ly in his "remarkable novels."

3   BURNE, GLENN S. <u>Remy de Gourmont: His Ideas and Influences
    in England and America</u>. Carbondale, Illinois: Southern
    Illinois Univ. Press, pp. 9, 12, 13, 14, 16.
        In 1884, through Villiers de l'Isle-Adam, Gourmont met
    Huysmans, "whose <u>A Rebours</u> was to be reflected in Gour-
    mont's work for the next decade." Huysmans became "the
    most important literary influence of Gourmont's early
    years." Through Gourmont, Huysmans met Berthe de Cour-
    rière, "the original for . . . Mme. Chantelouve in <u>Là-Bas</u>."
    Huysmans wrote the preface to Gourmont's <u>Le Latin mystique</u>,
    in which Huysmans attacked "the pseudo-mysticism of the
    nineteenth century" and displayed "his growing lack of
    sympathy for the Symbolist movement."

4   CONNOLLY, CYRIL. "Huysmans," in his <u>Previous Convictions</u>.
    London: Hamish Hamilton; New York: Harper & Row,
    pp. 202-204.
        Reprint of 1955.7.

5   CUMMINGS, RICHARD J. "The Role of Suffering in the Works of
    Joris-Karl Huysmans." Doctoral dissertation, Stanford
    University.

6   ENTREMONT, ELAINE D'. "The Influence of Joris-Karl Huysmans'
    <u>A Rebours</u> on Ruben Dario." <u>Romance Notes</u>, 5 (Autumn),
    37-40.
        <u>A Rebours</u> greatly influenced the Spanish "Modernistas,"
    especially Dario. The "correspondences" of the "mouth
    organ" and Des Esseintes' comments on contemporary French
    literature found their way into Dario's early poetry.

7   FREEDMAN, RALPH. <u>The Lyrical Novel: Studies in Herman Hesse,
    André Gide, and Virginia Woolf</u>. Princeton: Princeton
    Univ. Press, pp. 35-38, 125, 155, 275.
        In writing <u>A Rebours</u>, Huysmans broke the naturalistic
    formula, but produced one in which the form "echoes the
    romantic pilgrimage toward a transcendence of the world of
    the sense at the same time it represents its denial." He
    dealt with the profound conflict between the Christian
    ethic and Schopenhauer's negative alternative. <u>A Rebours</u>
    is an extended prose poem--"a disguised lyric"--in which

"the hero reduces all other persons to objects and trans-
forms even his visions into things, life into form."

8   MAGILL, FRANK N., ed. Cyclopedia of Literary Characters. New
     York: Harper & Row, pp. 13-14, 300-301.
          Brief identifications of the principal characters in
     A Rebours and Là-Bas.

9   SCHWAB, ARNOLD T. James Gibbons Huneker: Critic of the Seven
     Arts. Stanford: Stanford Univ. Press, pp. 77-78, 80, 86,
     96, 141-42, 243, 261, 264, 269.
          Notes the heavy influence of Huysmans on Huneker. In
     A Rebours, Huysmans expressed ideas that later formed the
     nucleus of Huneker's critical theories. The Huysmans'
     touch is especially evident in his story "Where the Black
     Mass Was Heard." "Painted Veils" also owes "something to
     . . . Là-Bas and A Rebours."

10   SHEPPARD, LANCELOT. "Spectacular Convert." Tablet [London],
     217 (7 December), 1322, 1324.
          Review of H. R. T. Brandreth's Huysmans (see 1963.3):
     "a useful and enlightening account of Huysmans' works."
     The author's pessimism, his preoccupation with l'éternelle
     bêtise de l'homme, his exaggerated "dolorism," his pene-
     trating insights emerge clearly from this study.

1964

1   BEEBE, MAURICE. Ivory Towers and Sacred Founts: The Artist
     as Hero in Fiction from Goethe to Joyce. New York: New
     York Univ. Press, pp. 115, 139, 142, 144-47, 154, 157,
     158-59, 246.
          Huysmans reflected most of the literary tendencies of
     his day and did much to popularize them. His A Rebours be-
     came "a guidebook for esthetes." Baudelaire managed to be
     "a religious visionary, dandy, and demon simultaneously";
     Huysmans was one of the first writers "to follow the well-
     travelled route from dandyism to demonism to religious sal-
     vation." Là-Bas, En Route, La Cathédrale, and L'Oblat are
     his tetralogy that record his journey.

2   GREEN, FREDERICK C. French Novelists: From the Revolution to
     Proust. New York: Frederick Ungar, pp. 286, 287-88, 298,
     304.
          Reprint of 1931.3.

1964

3 LHOMBREAUD, ROGER. <u>Arthur Symons</u>. Philadelphia: Dufour,
   pp. 66-68, 72, 74, 98, 99, 162, 180-81, 290.
       Symons' early interest in Huysmans and visits made by
   Symons and Havelock Ellis when in Paris to see the author
   of <u>A Rebours</u> are related. Notes that Symons planned to
   dedicate his <u>Symbolist Movement</u> (<u>see</u> 1899.6) to Yeats, and
   in a letter to Yeats dated June 11, 1899 informs him that
   he is adding the chapter "Huysmans as a Symbolist" to the
   study; and that Huysmans' conversion has made Symons think
   about his own concept of the world, life, and the place of
   the artist in the scheme of things.

4 MAGILL, FRANK N., ed. <u>Masterplots: European Fiction Series</u>.
   New York: Salem Press, pp. 9, 258.
       Plot summaries of <u>A Rebours</u> and <u>Là-Bas</u>.

5 MATTHEWS, J. H. "<u>En Rade</u> and Huysmans' Departure from Naturalism." <u>L'Esprit Createur</u>, 4 (Summer), 84-93.
       In <u>En Rade</u> there is a mingling of dream and reality. As
   an inversion of Naturalism, the novel practiced surrealis-
   tic methods involuntarily. The atmosphere of the work is
   insistently depressing: "it pictures humanity as so un-
   relievedly depraved that in <u>En Rade</u> Huysmans has undertaken
   a virtuoso performance in which he displays skills practiced in his earlier novels, but only now brought to per-
   fection and exploited to the full." If the novel is a
   failure, it is not "a sterile failure." <u>En Rade</u> confirms
   Huysmans' departure from Naturalism and leads him to write
   <u>Là-Bas</u>.
       Reprinted: 1964.6 and in an expanded version in
   1966.16.

6 MATTHEWS, J. H. "J.-K. Huysmans: <u>En Rade</u>," in his <u>Surrealism
   and the Novel</u>. Ann Arbor: Univ. of Michigan Press,
   pp. 28-40.
       Reprint of 1964.5.

7 SWART, KOENRAAD W. <u>The Sense of Decadence in Nineteenth-
   Century France</u>. The Hague: M. Nijhoff, pp. 163-64, 165,
   166, 167, 248.
       <u>A Rebours</u> was "the greatest literary sensation in many
   years and became the real breviary of the Decadent Movement." Many individuals served as model for Des Esseintes:
   Baudelaire, Edmond de Goncourt, Comte de Montesquiou-
   Fesenzac, and Huysmans himself. The novel left a deep impression on many authors, especially Mallarmé and Valéry in
   France; Moore and Wilde in England.

8   TINSLEY, SISTER LUCY. "The 'Springboards' of Joris-Karl Huys-
    mans." L'Esprit Createur, 4 (Summer), 94–101.
        Huysmans' uniquely colorful language gives clues to his
    personality. The word tremplin (along with élan, jailler,
    éclater and other terms that reinforce the image of a
    springboard in action) has special significance when stud-
    ied in the context of his diction. Many examples can be
    culled to demonstrate application of the tremplin metaphor,
    which suggests that a foremost tendency of Huysmans' men-
    tality was to think and act in ways suggestive of the
    springboard and associated images.

9   VERLAINE, PAUL. Selected Poems. Translated with notes by
    C. F. MacIntyre. Berkeley: Univ. of California Press,
    pp. xiii, 214.
        Quotes Des Esseintes' words on Verlaine from Chapter XIV
    of A Rebours and Durtal's statement that "Verlaine gave the
    Catholic Church the only mystical verses since the Middle
    Ages" from Chapter II of La Cathédrale.

1965

1   BRAUN, SIDNEY D. "Huysmans, Joris-Karl," in Dictionary of
    French Literature. Totowa, N.J.: Littlefield, Adams,
    pp. 158–59.
        Reprint of 1958.4.

2   BRERETON, GEOFFREY. A Short History of French Literature.
    London: Penguin, pp. 128, 226, 228–29, 232.
        Reprint of 1954.7

3   CEVASCO, G. A. "En Route," in Masterpieces of Catholic Lit-
    erature. Edited by Frank N. Magill. New York: Salem
    Press, pp. 716–20.
        A summary of the novel with comments on its principal
    ideas is given. Emphasis is placed on the fact that ninety
    percent or more of the work is autobiographical. States
    why Huysmans chose the form of a novel instead of straight
    biography. The chief character, Durtal, endures agony of
    the spirit during an existential period before his conver-
    sion. After his "Night Obscure" during a retreat at a
    Trappist monastery, he embraces the Faith. Observations
    of monastic life, church art and architecture, the liturgy
    and plain chant, impress Durtal-Huysmans with their place
    in divine worship.

1965

4   FRIERSON, WILLIAM C.   The English Novel in Transition, 1885–
    1940. New York: Cooper Square, pp. x, 60-61, 69, 75, 76,
    77, 79, 190, 201, 207, 235, 260.
        Two major influences transformed the English novel:
    naturalism and "'spiritual naturalism,' as it appeared in
    Huysmans' writings and was later to affect England through
    Jean Christophe." Before Romain Rolland wrote Jean Chri-
    stophe, "he had profited from Huysmans' intensity and dis-
    cursiveness, but more from Huysmans' theories of fiction."
    Moore admired and imitated Huysmans' writings. Joyce, who
    read both Moore and Huysmans, was influenced by both in
    writing A Portrait of the Artist as a Young Man. Huysmans'
    influence is also found in Compton Mackenzie's Youth's En-
    counter and Sinister Street. With Huxley, as with Huys-
    mans, "the love of precise information becomes an aesthetic
    ideal"; but it was Huysmans "who seems to have discovered
    the charm of erudition in fiction."

5   JEROME, JOSEPH. Montague Summers: A Memoir. London: Cecil
    & Amelia Woolf, pp. 22, 54, 94.
        Summers had in him the makings of another Abbé Boullan,
    whom he knew a great deal about from reading Là-Bas [in
    which the Abbé is portrayed under the name of Doctor Jo-
    hannes]. In 1943, Summers supplied notes to a Fortune
    Press edition of Là-Bas; at the time he boasted that he was
    the only English member of the Société J.-K. Huysmans of
    Paris.

6   KRONEGGER, M. E. "Joyce's Debt to Poe and the French Symbol-
    ists." Revue de Littérature Comparée, no. 2 (Avril-Juin),
    pp. 243-54.
        Symons played a major role in introducing Joyce to Poe's
    works. More interested in Huysmans than any other Symbol-
    ist writer, Symons wrote of Des Esseintes' instinctive
    sympathy for Poe, as Huysmans had discussed it in detail in
    A Rebours. When Joyce read Huysmans' novel he was fasci-
    nated by Des Esseintes' aesthetic withdrawal, which had al-
    ready been idealized by Poe. Joyce, like another Poe-Des
    Esseintes, conceived of art "as a means of escape into a
    sphere of eternal beauty."

7   McGILL, V. J. August Strindberg: The Bedeviled Viking. New
    York: Russell & Russell, pp. 9, 375.
        When Strindberg first learned that Huysmans had accused
    Marquis Stanislaus de Guaita of black magic, he became
    "highly excited and indignant." He believed that he, like
    Huysmans, was a victim of evil. Strindberg particularly
    sympathized with Huysmans because, "as he learned from En
    Route, this writer had passed through just such a hell as
    his."

8   MASON, H. T.   "Huysmans."   Notes and Queries, 12 (February),
    75-77.
        Review of H. R. T. Brandreth's Huysmans (see 1963.3).
    With the renewed interest shown in Huysmans during the last
    few years, this short, general volume is welcome. For the
    uninitiated, "this little book is very satisfactory"; but
    for the reader "even a little conversant with the works of
    that strange imagination . . . it contains no new insights."

9   MORTENSER, BRITA M. E. and BRIAN W. DOWNS.   Strindberg: An
    Introduction to His Life and Work.   Cambridge: University
    Press, p. 169.
        Strindberg was influenced by Huysmans' Des Esseintes,
    especially in his depiction of Commissioner Borg, a dandy
    and an aesthete, in his novel In the Outer Skerries.

10 RAITT, A. W.   Life and Letters in France: The Nineteenth Cen-
    tury.   New York: Scribner's, pp. xxii, xxiv, 33, 86, 105,
    107, 125-26, 140, 142, 146, 147, 155.
        After writing A Rebours, in which the main character
    finds himself in a spiritual dilemma, Huysmans found his
    way to Catholicism via an interest in satanism and religious
    art. He became an important critic and theorist of paint-
    ing. He researched the phenomenon of diabolism to write
    Là-Bas, "a detailed account of Satanism in Parisian so-
    ciety." At the beginning of the novel, two characters
    argue about Naturalism; one praises the service which the
    Naturalists rendered to art; the other complains of their
    narrow, materialistic conception of human psychology.

1966

1   ALLEN, LOUIS.   "Letters of Huysmans and Zola to Raffalovich."
    Forum for Modern Language Study, 2 (July), 214-15.
        Marc-André Raffalovich addressed a questionnaire on
    homosexuality to Huysmans and a number of other French
    writers to gather information for a book he was writing on
    the subject [Uranisme et Unisexualité; 1896]. Huysmans'
    letters to Raffalovich, together with a brief note from
    Zola and a mere acknowledgement from Loti, are now kept in
    a leather portfolio at St. Dominic's Priory, George Square,
    Edinburgh. The article reprints these letters, numbered
    I-XI.

1966

2   BECKSON, KARL, ed. <u>Aesthetes and Decadents of the 1890's:</u>
     <u>An Anthology of British Poetry and Prose</u>. New York:
     Random House, Vintage Books, pp. xxvii-xxix, xxxii, xxxix.
          All the themes and images of the Decadence are found in
     <u>A Rebours</u>. The genius and delight of its sexually perverse
     hero, Des Esseintes, is to cultivate an interest in arti-
     fice and the abnormal. In his strange house outside Paris,
     he secludes himself from a hated bourgeois society to be
     absorbed "in the authors of the Latin Decadence, and exotic
     gems, diseased flowers and monstrous orchids that look
     artificial." Suffering boredom, he seeks sensations which
     are à rebours. English Decadents found Huysmans and his
     strange volume fascinating, but Pater, who was far less
     decadent than his disciples, is reported to have labelled
     the author of "the breviary of the Decadence" at best "a
     beastly man." Pater's hedonism was concerned with "the
     expansion and refinement of the power of perception."
     Wilde never grasped this, but he seems to have understood
     the motifs of Huysmans' <u>A Rebours</u>, which he used to good
     advantage in <u>Dorian Gray</u>.

3   BRERETON, GEOFFREY. <u>A Short History of French Literature</u>.
     London: Penguin, pp. 128, 226, 228-29, 232.
          Reprint of 1954.7.

4   BROMBERT, VICTOR. <u>The Novels of Flaubert</u>. Princeton, N.J.:
     Princeton Univ. Press, pp. 80, 121-22.
          In <u>A Rebours</u>, Huysmans granted Salammbô "a position of
     honor in the sophisticated library of Des Esseintes."

5   BUTLER, KATHLEEN T. <u>A History of French Literature</u>. Vol. II.
     New York: Russell & Russell, Atheneum House, 239, 319,
     320.
          Reprint of 1923.4.

6   CONNOLLY, CYRIL. <u>The Modern Movement: A Discussion of One</u>
     <u>Hundred Books from England, France and America, 1850-1950</u>.
     New York: Atheneum, pp. 6, 13, 22.
          The Modern Movement is defined as "a revolt against the
     bourgeois in France, the Victorian in England, the puri-
     tanism and materialism of America" in books "with outstand-
     ing originality and richness of texture . . . with the
     spark of rebellion alight." In France, "Mallarmé and
     Huysmans almost created the modern sensibility between
     them." <u>A Rebours</u> is "a key book" for many reasons, one
     being Des Esseintes' library, "particularly its modern sec-
     tion which is uncannily prescient of our taste today."
     Huysmans' novel did not so much advance literary tastes as

create them. As for La-Bas, this is Huysmans' "greatest
novel," though Surrealists may prefer En Rade "on account
of some vitriolic sequences by this Swiftian expert on
discomfort."

7   CROSLAND, MARGARET, ed. A Guide to Literary Europe.
    Vol. III. Philadelphia and New York: Chilton Books, 28,
    40, 44, 88, 91.
        Refers to such geographical locations and sites asso-
    ciated with Huysmans as Chartres (La Cathédrale), Lourdes
    (Les Foules de Lourdes), Médan ("Sac au dos" in Les Soirées
    de Médan), No. 9 Rue Suger in Paris (the house in which
    Huysmans was born), and the Parisian church of Saint Sul-
    pice (mentioned in La-Bas).

8   GOURMONT, REMY DE. Selected Writings. Translated and edited
    by Glenn S. Burne. Ann Arbor, Mich.: Univ. of Michigan
    Press, pp. 73, 187, 216, 221.
        Symbolism as a movement "acquired all its force when
    some young poets guided by a famous chapter in Huysmans'
    A Rebours and discovering Mallarmé and Verlaine at the same
    time, found themselves enthusiastic and, so to speak, fec-
    undated on the spot."

9   GRANT, ELLIOT M. Emile Zola. New York: Twayne, pp. 71, 73,
    84, 100-101, 168.
        During the 1870s, Zola saw a great deal of his young
    disciples Huysmans, Céard, Alexis, Hennique, and Maupas-
    sant. Each of the five agreed to write a story on the
    Franco-Prussian War to be published in a single volume.
    They chose the title Les Soirées de Médan to render homage
    to the hospitality they had enjoyed at Zola's country
    house. Huysmans' contribution was "Sac au Dos." Among
    all Zola's novels, Huysmans regarded L'Assommoir as Zola's
    "extraordinary achievement."

10 GRIFFITHS, R. The Reactionary Revolution. New York: Fred-
    erick Ungar, pp. 104-109.
        Huysmans came to accept a religion of suffering far
    from the aesthetic delights of a fin-de-siècle dilettante,
    but he was a target for all those critical of aesthetic
    Catholicism. He loved beauty in Church art when it was
    compatible with his aesthetic sensibility; for him the
    main thing was the meaning of art in religious terms. In
    his view, a Matthaeus Grunewald crucifixion contained more
    impact than any other work of religious art.

1966

11 HEMMINGS, F. W. J. <u>Emile Zola</u>. Oxford: Clarendon Press,
      pp. 109, 117, 137, 142, 160, 166-69, 173, 183, 231, 247,
      264, 268.
        Reprint of 1953.6 in an enlarged edition.

12 HOLT, ELIZABETH GILMORE, ed. <u>From the Classicists to the Im-</u>
      <u>pressionists: Art and Architecture in the Nineteenth Cen-</u>
      <u>tury</u>. Vol. III of <u>A Documentary History of Art</u>. New York:
      Archer Books, Doubleday, 389, 481-89, 496, 502.
        Brief biographical sketch with a focus on <u>A Rebours</u>,
      <u>L'Art moderne</u>, and <u>Certains</u>. As a critic of <u>Salons</u> and Ex-
      positions (1879-1881), Huysmans was brought into close as-
      sociation with such artists as Moreau and Redon, "whose
      interests in the reality of the imaged world paralleled
      his own and led to the development of symbolism." Whistler,
      upon his move to Paris in 1892, was not especially popular
      with the majority of French writers, but he was admired by
      Huysmans. Gaugin shared with Verlaine, Mallarmé, and Huys-
      mans the desire "to escape contemporary life by flight to
      the remote and symbolic." In his <u>Certains</u> Huysmans "cor-
      rectly discerned the genius of Degas, Whistler, Renoir, and
      other Impressionists."

13 IGNOTUS, PAUL. <u>The Paradox of Maupassant</u>. London: Univ. of
      London Press, pp. 101, 123, 127, 131, 177, 181, 188, 262.
        Maupassant's young friends were such writers as Huysmans,
      Céard, Hennique, and Alexis--all admirers of Zola, with whom
      they formed a literary circle. Later, in a conflict that
      Maupassant had with Edmond de Goncourt, Huysmans apparently
      sided with Goncourt, as the latter noted in his <u>Journal</u>.

14 JACKSON, HOLBROOK. <u>The Eighteen Nineties: A Review of Art</u>
      <u>and Ideas at the Close of the Nineteenth Century</u>. New
      York: Capricorn Books, G. P. Putnam's Sons, pp. 28, 58,
      61, 63, 136, 223.
        Reprint of 1913.2.

15 LAWRENCE, JULIE BROOKS. "Mallarmé and Des Esseintes." Mas-
      ter's thesis, Columbia University.

16 MATTHEWS, J. H. "J.-K. Huysmans," in his <u>Surrealism and the</u>
      <u>novel</u>. Ann Arbor, Mich.: Univ. of Michigan Press,
      pp. 28-40.
        Surrealists single out Huysmans' work for special com-
      mendation. In <u>En Rade</u>, he practiced surrealist methods in-
      voluntarily; yet the results obtained are completely valid
      for surrealism.
        Reprint of 1964.6 in an expanded version.

17   READ, HERBERT, ed. "Huysmans, Joris-Karl," in <u>Encyclopedia of
      the Arts</u>. New York: Meredith Press, p. 413.
         Biographical entry. Lists Huysmans' best known works
      and labels <u>A Rebours</u> "a representative book of the 'deca-
      dent' spirit . . . widely imitated."

<u>1967</u>

1   BART, BENJAMIN F. <u>Flaubert</u>. Syracuse: Syracuse Univ. Press,
      pp. 349, 488, 628, 630, 631, 707, 720.
         Flaubert did not like the works of the young Naturalists
      Huysmans, Hennique, or Alexis, but he strove to wean them
      away from Zola. He invited them to his bachelor apartment
      on Sunday afternoons to discuss literature with them.
      Huysmans delighted in Flaubert's <u>La Tentation de Saint-
      Antoine</u>, but he found its author "painfully lacking in
      intelligence, even quite stupid on occasion."

2   BLUNT, H. F. "J.-K. Huysmans," in his <u>Great Penitents</u>.
      Freeport, N.Y.: Books for Libraries Press, pp. 169-90.
         Reprint of 1921.2.

3   BOWRA, C. M. <u>The Heritage of Symbolism</u>. New York: St. Mar-
      tin's Press; London: Macmillan, pp. 12-13, 222.
         The aesthetic withdrawal idealized by the Symbolists
      found "its complete expression in Des Esseintes, the hero
      of Huysmans' novel <u>A Rebours</u>. . . ."

4   BUSST, A. J. L. "The Image of the Androgyne in the Nineteenth
      Century," in <u>Romantic Mythologies</u>. Edited by Ian Fletcher.
      London: Routledge & Kegan Paul, pp. 5, 50, 53, 57-58, 74.
         <u>A Rebours</u> tells of Des Esseintes' infatuation for the
      American Miss Urania. He could not grasp the strange al-
      lurement until he realized that as he watched her night
      after night at the circus "she gradually changed in his
      mind from a woman, first to an indistinct androgyne, and
      finally to a complete man."

5   CEVASCO, G. A. "A Dose of Opium: J.-K. Huysmans' <u>A Rebours</u>."
      <u>American Book Collector</u>, 17 (April), 12-16.
         This article, whose title comes from George Moore's com-
      ment that "a page of Huysmans is as a dose of opium, a
      glass of exquisite and powerful liquor," examines the
      genesis, narrative, and style of <u>A Rebours</u>. Notes that
      the novel is "more than a delightful tidbit"; rather, it
      is "a masterpiece of French literature." Furthermore,

1967

A Rebours is both the key to the mind of a strange genius and the book that formulated the psychology of the Decadent Movement.

6   CHARVET, P. E.   A Literary History of France: The Nineteenth and Twentieth Centuries, 1870-1940.   London: Ernest Benn; New York: Barnes & Noble, pp. 29, 42-48, 63, 82, 114, 121, 163, 175, 199.
        In contrast to Zola's gigantic fresco efforts that his novels provide, Huysmans worked on a small canvas. To that extent the characters in his naturalistic novels "come alive in the reader's mind." Then, too, Huysmans always tended to identify with one or another of his characters. Des Esseintes, however, was "no more than a pale image, an intellectual fantasy," though he has "a significance that extends beyond Huysmans himself. "We can appreciate that, as Huysmans' own sense of spiritual dissatisfaction grew, he should feel the need to make a clear break with the neuropathic Des Esseintes and project his mood into a less shadowy character." This later identification is found in Durtal, the central figure in Là-Bas, En Route, La Cathédrale and L'Oblat. Durtal gives us chapters from Huysmans' own experience, "moments of the conflicts and pilgrimage that led him--and others of his generation--from spiritual darkness into the light of the Christian faith."

7   CURLEY, DOROTHY NYREN and ARTHUR CURLEY. "Huysmans, Joris-Karl," in their A Library of Literary Criticism: Modern Romance Literature. New York: Unger, pp. 227-29.
        Brief excerpts from various studies of Huysmans by such writers as George Moore (see 1888.1), Arthur Symons (see 1919.7), Robert Baldick (see 1955.3), A. E. Carter (see 1958.5), and John Senior (see 1959.8).

8   GOLDEN, B.   "'That Brute' Courbet and Realism."   Criticism, 9 (Winter), 22-41.
        Huysmans, writing to a friend, referred to Courbet as "that brute" and "apostle of realism." This reference was symptomatic of the profound disruption of the historical continuity of art that took place in the nineteenth century.

9   GOURMONT, REMY DE.   "Huysmans," in his The Book of Masks. Translated by Jack Lewis. Freeport, N.Y.:   Books for Libraries Press, pp. 195-201.
        Reprint of 1921.4.

10 JULLIAN, PHILIPPE. The Collectors. Translated by M. Callum.
    London: Sidgwick & Jackson, pp. 58-62.
       Huysmans' Des Esseintes in the novel A Rebours had one
    of the most fantastic collections of art ever assembled
    under one roof, his chateau at Fontenay. Most collections
    offer distractions from the humdrum of life, but even with
    his barricade of art and books Des Esseintes could not es-
    cape from boredom.

11 M[oore]-R[involucci], M.[ina] J.[osephine]. "Huysmans, Joris-
    Karl," in Chambers's Encyclopedia. Vol. VII. London,
    Toronto, and New York: Pergamon Press, 324.
       Biographical entry. "A leading naturalist writer,"
    Huysmans turned to analyses of Impressionist paintings,
    dabbled in the occult, and underwent a spiritual pilgrimage
    which brought him back to the church.

12 PEYRE, HENRI. French Novelists of Today. New York: Oxford
    Univ. Press, pp. 13, 25, 269, 379.
       Huysmans "deserves to return to popularity, more so, in
    our eyes, than do Léon Bloy or Barbey d'Aurevilly, two
    Catholic but uncharitable souls and novelists of some
    power."

13 REID, RANDALL. The Fiction of Nathanael West. Chicago:
    Univ. of Chicago Press, pp. 24-27.
       Discusses Là-Bas and En Route as sources for West's The
    Dream Life of Balso Snell.

14 THIBAUDET, ALBERT. French Literature from 1795 to Our Era.
    Translated by Charles Lam Markmann. New York: Funk & Wag-
    nalls, pp. 334, 335, 336, 391, 409, 410, 428.
       As a naturalist, Huysmans had a style of his own "far
    superior and even opposite to Zola's in its quest for new
    expression. . . ." A Rebours made him famous; but except
    for that novel, "he never wrote anything but the biography
    of a dyspeptic and maniacal bachelor, sometimes on the hunt
    for a quiet restaurant (A Vau-l'Eau), sometimes in the bore-
    dom of a miserable vacation (En Rade), sometimes in quest
    of the devil (Là-Bas), and finally in search of God (En
    Route, La Cathédrale, L'Oblat)."

15 TINSLEY, LUCY. "Huysmans, Joris-Karl," in New Catholic En-
    cyclopedia. Vol. VII. New York: McGraw-Hill, 279-80.
       Biographical entry. Huysmans' appeal has been limited
    but his popularity "is slowly increasing." Impressionism
    and symbolism owe much of their reputation to his praise of
    them.

1967

16 WADE, CLAIRE B. "Sentence Structure and Sensory Imagery in
    the Novels of Joris-Karl Huysmans." Doctoral dissertation,
    University of Michigan.

17 WARD-JACKSON, PHILIP. "Art Historians and Art Critics VIII:
    Huysmans." Burlington Magazine, 109 (November), 617-22.
       Art meant a great deal to Huysmans "as a backcloth to
    his literary activities." As a critic he was most im-
    pressed by artists who displayed originality. He espe-
    cially admired the paintings of the Dutch Masters, the
    Impressionists, and the "mystical naturalism" of Grunewald.
    Huysmans expressed his views on art with vigor in A Re-
    bours, En Ménage, Là-Bas, and Certains.

18 W.[einer], S.[eymour] S. "Huysmans, Charles Marie Georges,"
    in European Authors, 1000-1900. New York: H. W. Wilson,
    pp. 437-39.
       Bio-critical entry. Refers to A Rebours as "the best
    known of Huysmans' works." Notes that his Oeuvres Com-
    plètes was edited by Lucien Descaves and published in
    twenty-three volumes (1928-34).

19 WEINREB, RUTH PLAUT. "Joris-Karl Huysmans' A Rebours: A
    Study of Structure, Metaphor and Artifice." Doctoral dis-
    sertation, Columbia University.

1968

1   CURRAN, C. P. James Joyce Remembered. London: Oxford Univ.
    Press, pp. 28-29.
       Huysmans' deification of art and his utilization of
    color and synaesthetic fancies of taste, sound, and smell
    in A Rebours made an impact upon the young Joyce. The au-
    thor of The Portrait of the Artist as a Young Man found
    "absolute value: a world of integrated beauty" in the
    aestheticism of Des Esseintes.

2   ELLIS, HAVELOCK. From Rousseau to Proust. Freeport, N.Y.:
    Books for Libraries Press, pp. 5, 11-13, 174, 269, 313,
    324, 380, 394.
       Reprint of 1935.2.

3   GRIFFITHS, RICHARD. "Reviews." French Studies, 22 (April),
    176.
       Review of J.-K. Huysmans: Lettres Inédites à Jules
    Destrée; edited by G. Vanwelkenhuzen (Genève: Droz; Paris:
    Minard, 1967): "in the best tradition of Huysmans' schol-
    arship, with copious notes which explain the subjects

treated in the letters themselves, and with an excellent introduction placing their recipient." These letters have been chosen because they give information about the literary life of Belgium at the time, they contain valuable discussions of art and artists, and they present many examples of acute criticism of contemporary writers.

4 GRUBBS, HENRY A. <u>Paul Valéry</u>. New York: Twayne, pp. 18, 23, 33.

In 1891, Valéry first met Huysmans, "whose <u>A Rebours</u> he admired so much." Through Huysmans' novel, Valéry discovered Verlaine and Mallarmé. In 1895, following the advice of Huysmans, Valéry entered the competition for a position in the War Office.

5 HARGREAVES-MAWDSLEY, W. N. <u>Everyman's Dictionary of European Writers</u>. London: J. M. Dent; New York: Dutton, pp. 270-71.

Biographical entry. States the influence of Baudelaire, Zola, and the Goncourts on Huysmans. Lists his principal works. Labels <u>A Rebours</u> "his masterpiece." Huysmans' style was one "of extreme originality."

6 NIESS, ROBERT J. <u>Zola, Cézanne, and Manet: A Study of L'Oeuvre</u>. Ann Arbor: Univ. of Michigan Press, pp. 19, 66, 153, 187-88, 247.

Possibly certain themes in Huysmans' <u>En Ménage</u> take their departure from Zola's <u>L'Oeuvre</u>. In 1885, Zola as a critic of art was as "modern" as Huysmans, though few other observers of the art scene were. Zola once remarked to Huysmans, who highly admired the work of Degas, that Degas was a "<u>constipé du plus talent</u>."

7 MAGILL, FRANK N. <u>Masterplots: Comprehensive Library Edition</u>. New York: Salem Press, pp. 50, 1263.

Plot summaries of <u>A Rebours</u> and <u>Là-Bas</u>.

8 RIDGE, GEORGE ROSS. <u>Joris-Karl Huysmans</u>. New York: Twayne, 123 pp.

Huysmans is "the archetypal Decadent." In his early work he was a naturalist and later evolved into a Catholic writer. Chapter I is mainly a biographical sketch. The second chapter focuses on the young Huysmans as a naturalist. His middle period is considered in Chapter III and contains a discussion of his "decadence." The aging Huysmans, who experiences a profound conversion after a lengthy spiritual crisis, is the subject of Chapter IV. The conclusion, Chapter V, summarizes the meaning and importance of Huysmans' work "in the context of the

1968

Decadent world view." The significance of his Decadent
philosophy to our own age gives Huysmans, "one of the most
complex men of his time," his peculiar and abiding reputation. Today, "the very name of Joris-Karl Huysmans incarnates the decadent fin de siècle with more brilliance than
that of any other writer of the glittering age."

9   SEWELL, BROCARD. <u>Footnote to the Nineties: A Memoir of John
     Gray and André Raffalovich</u>. London: Cecil & Amelia Woolf,
     pp. 5, 12, 51, 58, 69.
         Both Gray and Raffalovich were devotees of Huysmans.
     One of Gray's earliest published articles was on En Route
     and Là-Bas; it appeared in The Dial (see 1896.6). Raffa-
     lovich's special joy was his library, especially the latest
     French novels and works of criticism: "He possessed every
     edition, or nearly so, of the works of J.-K. Huysmans."

10   SHAPIRO, KARL. <u>To Abolish Children and Other Essays</u>. Chicago:
     Quadrangle Books, p. 219.
         Among 1400 books of poetry collected by Shapiro over the
     years are the novels of Huysmans: "I keep [them] for theo-
     retical substantiation of some of the things that happened
     to poetry just before our time."

11   SPRAGUE, CLAIRE. <u>Edgar Saltus</u>. New York: Twayne, pp. 42, 53,
     55, 67, 68, 71, 81, 119, 123, 136.
         Huysmans' influence is apparent in several works of
     Saltus, especially the novels When Dreams Come True, En-
     thralled, and Mr. Incoul's Misadventure, as well as the
     essay "Fashions in Poisons." Saltus admired Huysmans, but
     "the Huysmans style--'high-flavored and spotted with cor-
     ruption'-- . . . is not the Saltus style."

12   VALÉRY, PAUL. "Recollections of J.-K. Huysmans" and "Durtal,"
     in his <u>Masters and Friends</u>. Translated by Martin Turnell.
     Princeton, N.J.: Princeton Univ. Press, pp. 265-68,
     269-83.
         In his "Recollections," Valéry states that he had a spe-
     cial fondness for the author of A Rebours. He admired
     Huysmans' erudition, his literary style. In "Durtal,"
     Valéry traces the character who gives unity to Là-Bas, En
     Route, and La Cathédrale--"three books which alone have
     brought something generally new to the contemporary novel."

1969

1 ANDERSON, W. "Huysmans, Georges Charles," in <u>Penguin Compan-</u>
   <u>ion to European Literature</u>. Edited by A. Thorlby. New
   York: McGraw-Hill, p. 382.
      Biographical entry. Huysmans' name has become "a syno-
   nym for decadence," but he also wrote art criticism and
   was "one of the first to appreciate the Impressionists."

2 ANON. "Dedicated Decadent." <u>MD</u> (November), pp. 231-37.
      Huysmans went to "the depths of despair and pessimism,
   then turned from the edge of the abyss to a faith imbued
   with the spirit of hope and the tranquil acceptance of suffering." <u>A Rebours</u> is the keystone of his life and work.
   As a writer, he dedicated his life to art and truth. His
   interest in dreams and his extensive use of comparisons and
   terms taken from medicine have made him a favorite of
   French physicians for over fifty years.

3 BRADY, PATRICK. "Reviews." <u>French Review</u>, 42 (April), 768.
      Review of George Ross Ridge's <u>Joris-Karl Huysmans</u> (<u>see</u>
   1968.8). Organized with simplicity and clarity, this
   study provides a good and painless introduction to the
   life and work of a writer "of considerable aesthetic interest and no small historical importance."

4 CARTER, A. E. <u>Verlaine: A Study in Parallels</u>. Toronto:
   Univ. of Toronto, pp. 193, 208.
      <u>A Rebours</u> did a great deal to establish Verlaine's
   reputation.

5 CEVASCO, G. A. "Book Reviews." <u>Modern Language Journal</u>, 53
   (January), 35-36.
      Review of George Ross Ridge's <u>Joris-Karl Huysmans</u> (<u>see</u>
   1968.8). Focuses on the one writer who "incarnates the
   decadent <u>fin de siècle</u> with more brilliance than that of
   any other writer of the glittering age." One could be
   captious about certain judgments rendered and could easily
   carp about the disproportionate attention accorded some aspects of Huysmans' work and denied others, but the study
   should prove useful to students and devotees of French
   letters.

6 CEVASCO, G. A. "Reviews." <u>Books Abroad</u>, 43 (Spring), 227.
      Review of George Ross Ridge's <u>Joris-Karl Huysmans</u> (<u>see</u>
   1968.8). A useful addition to the growing number of studies that are appearing in English, this bio-critical study

explores and analyzes Huysmans' major works. A final chapter summarizes the meaning and the importance of Huysmans' books "in the context of the Decadent World View."

7   CRUICKSHANK, JOHN. French Literature and Its Backgrounds: The Late Nineteenth Century. London, Oxford, and New York: Oxford Univ. Press, pp. 11, 12, 178, 179, 180, 194, 195, 196-97.
Brief discussions of Huysmans' aesthetic preoccupations and his place in the Catholic literary revival. Focuses in particular on Là-Bas, En Route, La Cathédrale, and L'Oblat.

8   ELLIS, HAVELOCK. "Huysmans," in his The New Spirit. Mamaroneck, N.Y.: Kraus Reprint, pp. 219-70.
Reprint of 1898.15.

9   ELLIS, HAVELOCK. Introduction to John Howard's translation of A Rebours. New York: Dover, pp. v-xxxii.
Reprint of 1898.15.

10 ENGLER, WINFRIED. The French Novel from Eighteen Hundred to the Present. Translated by Alexander Gode. New York: Frederick Ungar, pp. 79, 85, 91, 94, 98-103, 109, 159, 218, 230, 242.
In the work of Huysmans, fin-de-siècle literature appears "concentrate exemplarily." The principle of "a rebours" runs as a common thread through all his books.

11 HATZFELD, HELMUT A. Literature Through Art: A New Approach to French Literature. Chapel Hill: Univ. of North Carolina Press, p. 158.
Huysmans disliked Millet's Angelus: "These peasants are as conventional, as fictitious as the 'Petites Fadettes' and the 'Champis' invented by that old spinner of of the ideal called George Sand."

12 HICKS, GRANVILLE. Figures of Transition: A Study of British Literature at the End of the Nineteenth Century. Westport, Conn.: Greenwood Press, pp. 254-58.
Reprint of 1939.1.

13 JONES, W. GLYN. Johannes Jorgensen. New York: Twayne, pp. 18, 25, 44.
In 1892, A Rebours served as a model for Jorgensen in his writing of the novel Sommer. An inscription he wrote inside the front cover of Trois Eglises et Trois Primitifs in 1908--and later pasted over--reveals the turmoil of his mind when he thought of himself as another Huysmans "in God's grindstone."

14   JOSEPHSON, MATTHEW. <u>Zola and His Time</u>. New York: Russell &
         Russell, pp. 222, 224, 225, 240, 260, 265, 266, 268-72,
         283, 286, 309, 317, 355, 357, 358, 383.
            Reprint of 1928.4.

15   JULLIAN, PHILIPPE. <u>Oscar Wilde</u>. Translated by Violet Wyndham.
         London: Constable; New York: Viking, pp. 3, 217-218.
            Wilde's debt to Huysmans was immense, and Wilde acknowl-
         edged it. When someone asked Wilde about the genesis of
         <u>Dorian Gray</u>, he responded that it was "partly suggested by
         Huysmans' <u>A Rebours</u>, which you can get at any French book-
         seller." It is obvious that the references to jewels and
         perfumes are straight out of Huysmans' "poisonous book" in
         a yellow cover that Lord Henry makes Dorian read. "The
         Duc Floressas des Esseintes is . . . the father of Dorian
         Gray. . . ."

16   KAHN, ANNETTE. "Review." <u>Modern Language Review</u>, 64
         (October), 908-909.
            Review of J.-K. Huysmans: <u>Lettres Inédites à Jules
         Destrée</u>; edited by G. Vanwelkenhuzen (Genève: Droz; Paris:
         Minard, 1967). Huysmans was not an enthusiastic or par-
         ticularly gifted letter writer; his missives do not rank
         among the best in French literature. Usually short, honest,
         and to the point, they give a vivid first-hand picture of
         the writer: "ill at ease in the world he lived in, in-
         creasingly at odds with the literary climate of the day,
         struggling to get his works finished and published, and
         constantly fighting ill health."

17   MERRIT, JAMES DOUGLAS. <u>Ronald Firbank</u>. New York: Twayne,
         pp. 31-32, 55.
            Firbank burlesqued Huysmans' style and subject matter
         several times in his witty works of fiction. In <u>Vainglory</u>,
         there is an elaborate description of a room belonging to
         Lady Georgia Blueharnis delightfully reminiscent of one of
         Des Esseintes' art-filled rooms at Fontenay. Other such
         parodies allow the inference that Firbank knew <u>A Rebours</u>
         well.

18   MUNRO, JOHN M. <u>Arthur Symons</u>. New York: Twayne, pp. 30, 37,
         39-40, 42, 66, 78, 98, 120, 134.
            In 1899, Symons first journeyed to Paris to meet the
         leaders of the younger literary generation: Huysmans,
         Mallarmé, Gourmont, and others. Huysmans was one of his
         early favorites; his work was "so fascinating, so repel-
         lent, so instinctively artificial" that it represented "the
         main tendencies, the chief results of the Decadent Movement
         in literature." Unwilling to commit himself completely,

1969

Symons did concede that A Rebours, in spite of its strange-
ness and charm, is "undoubtedly the expression of a personality as remarkable as that of any contemporary writer's."

19   ROSSMAN, E. D. "From the Secular Meal to the Holy Table: The
     Problem of Food in the Fiction of Joris-Karl Huysmans."
     Doctoral dissertation, Rochester University.

20   SANDIFORD-PELLÉ, J. W. G. Introduction to his translation of
     En Ménage. London: Fortune Press, pp. 7-14.
          Gives brief biography of Huysmans, discusses his early
     works, and gives a detailed analysis of the context and
     significance of En Ménage. The novel caused a sensation
     when published in 1881 because it went "beyond the normal
     bounds of . . . subject and form in laying bare human emo-
     tions, sex and soul in a new style." The prose is "as
     evocative as Baudelaire's poetry." Of great interest as a
     human and historical document, this "song of nihilism" de-
     picts "the vital phases of the aesthetic, spiritual, intel-
     lectual, moral and real life of late nineteenth-century
     France."

21   STURM, FRANK PEARCE. Life, Letters, and Collected Works.
     Edited by Richard Taylor. Chicago: Univ. of Illinois
     Press, pp. 52, 127.
          Notes among the books that influenced his life, En
     Route, La Cathédrale, and L'Oblat: "In my youth I read
     them in French, but . . . I like translations better than
     the originals." An interest in the paintings of Moreau
     was a consequence of his reading of Huysmans' A Rebours.

22   SYMONS, ARTHUR. "Joris-Karl Huysmans," in his Figures of
     Several Centuries. Freeport, N.Y.: Books for Libraries
     Press, pp. 268-99.
          Reprint of 1916.3.

23   WEINBERG, KURT. "Huysmans, Joris-Karl," in Encyclopedia of
     World Literature in the Twentieth Century. Edited by Wolf-
     gang Bernard Fleischmann. Vol. III. New York: Ungar,
     128-29.
          Bio-critical entry. Apart from a short stay in 1899 as
     a lay brother in the Benedictine monastery of Liguge, Huys-
     mans all his life was "an inveterate Parisian, a dandy in
     the Baudelairean sense, and a gripping, ironic portrayer
     of certain seamy sides of modern city life."

112

1970

24 WRIGHT, C. H. C. <u>A History of French Literature</u>. New York:
     Haskell House, pp. 767, 774, 775, 776-77, 801, 803, 859,
     883.
          Reprint of 1912.2.

1970

1   BA.[LDICK], R.[OBERT]. "Huysmans, Joris-Karl," in <u>Encyclope-
     dia Britannica</u>. Vol. XI. Chicago, London, Toronto, etc.:
     William Benton, 919-20.
          Bio-critical entry. "The chief interest and importance
     of Huysmans' novels . . . lies in their autobiographical
     quality." A brief analysis of all his novels is given.

2   BEARDSLEY, AUBREY. <u>The Letters of Aubrey Beardsley</u>. Edited
     by Henry Maas, J. L. Duncan, and W. G. Good. Rutherford,
     N.J.: Fairleigh Univ. Press, pp. 257, 302, 434.
          In a letter to André Raffalovich dated February 24, 1897,
     Beardsley refers to Huysmans' "new work," <u>La Cathédrale</u>.
     In another letter to Raffalovich dated April 13, 1897,
     Beardsley thanks him for arranging a meeting with Huysmans
     in Paris. [There is no evidence that the meeting took
     place.] In a third letter to Raffalovich dated February 21,
     1898, Beardsley mentions that he read a short extract of
     <u>La Cathédrale</u> "in some paper which made me curious to get
     the book, but I don't expect to like it as I never like
     Huysmans."

3   CHIARI, JOSEPH. <u>Symbolism from Poe to Mallarmé: The Growth
     of a Myth</u>. New York: Gordian Press, pp. 57, 60, 68.
          Allusions to <u>A Rebours</u> and the violent criticism it
     aroused when first published in 1884. Mallarmé's "La Prose
     pour Des Esseintes" is pervaded with a Poesque atmosphere;
     psychologically, Des Esseintes is closely associated with
     Roderick Usher.

4   CORNELL, KENNETH. <u>The Symbolist Movement</u>. Hamden, Conn.:
     Archon Books, pp. 13, 24, 26, 30, 32, 35, 40, 43, 60, 73,
     74, 79, 82, 91, 117, 193, 197.
          Reprint of 1951.3.

5   CRAWFORD, VIRGINIA. "J.-K. Huysmans," in her <u>Studies in For-
     eign Literature</u>. New York: Kennikat Press, pp. 78-105.
          Reprint of 1899.4.

1970

6   ELLIS, HAVELOCK. "Huysmans," in <u>Critics of the Nineties</u>.
        Edited by Derek Stanford. London: John Baker, pp. 142-71.
            Reprint of 1898.15.

7   ERICKSON, JOHN D. "Huysmans' Là-Bas: A Metaphor of Search."
        <u>French Review</u>, 43 (February), 418-25.
            Huysmans' "satanic book," Là-Bas, is a novel of search.
        Its hero, Durtal, a character torn by conflict between
        bodily and spiritual needs, is suspended between the mech-
        anism of sensation and the void of spirit. He suffers in
        a limbo for he has not rejected the base materialism of
        his fellow men; but he cannot succeed in replacing it with
        the spiritual ideal for which he longs. On a metaphoric
        level his life is the search of the medieval alchemist for
        the elusive philosopher's stone. The love Mme. Chantelouve
        inspires in him, like the fascination he feels for Gilles
        de Rais, evolves this analogy. Through his research into
        the life of Gilles de Rais, Durtal seeks to uncover lost
        secrets of the Middle Ages, reflective of the unity of the
        spiritual and the carnal. At the end of the novel, his
        search is still unresolved. The philosopher's stone stands
        in contrast to the positivist spirit of the modern age:
        the secrets of the Middle Ages are lost forever.

8   HAYMAN, DAVID. <u>Ulysses: The Mechanics of Meaning</u>. Engle-
        wood, N.J.: Prentice Hall, pp. 12-13.
            Joyce's early prose style reflects his wide reading.
        The mannered, elliptical style of <u>The Portrait of the Art-
        ist as a Young Man</u> "recalls Walter Pater, J.-K. Huysmans,
        and . . . Gabrielle D'Annunzio," especially since the novel
        is "larded with bits of aesthetic and philosophic asides."

9   HUNEKER, JAMES G. <u>Overtones, A Book of Temperaments</u>. Free-
        port, N.Y.: Books for Libraries Press, pp. 204-10. Re-
        print of 1904.2.

10   KASTNER, L. E. and HENRY GIBSON ATKINS. <u>A Short History of
        French Literature</u>. Port Washington, N.Y.: Kennikat Press,
        pp. 321-22.
            Reprint of 1925.2.

11   LAVRIN, JANKO. "Huysmans and Strindberg," in his <u>Studies in
        European Literature</u>. Port Washington, N.Y.: Kennikat
        Press, pp. 118-30.
            Reprint of 1929.4.

12 McKALIK, BENJAMIN M. "Archibald MacLeish and the French Sym-
      bolist Tradition [Mallarmé, Huysmans, Verlaine, Rimbaud,
      etc.]." Doctoral dissertation, University of South
      Carolina.

13 MEYER, LAURA K. "Temptress and Redemptress: The Place of
      Women in the Life and Works of Joris-Karl Huysmans." Mas-
      ter's thesis, Univ. of Louisville.

14 MUEHSAM, GERD, ed. French Painters and Painting from the
      Fourteenth Century to Post-Impressionism. New York:
      Frederick Ungar, pp. 377-78, 408-409, 424-25, 447-48, 451,
      462-63, 470, 486, 493, 523.
        Contains excerpts from criticism of Cézanne, Degas,
      Manet, Millet, Moreau, Morisot, Pissarro, Redon, and
      Sisley that appears in L'Art moderne, A Rebours, and
      Certains.

15 MUNRO, JOHN M. The Decadent Poetry of the Eighteen-Nineties.
      Beirut, Lebanon: American Univ. Press, pp. 55-56.
        Relates the significance of Huysmans to the English
      Decadence: "The most important influence of all was not a
      poet but a novelist, Joris-Karl Huysmans, whose A Rebours
      . . . gave many of the Decadents their raison d'être."

16 PRAZ, MARIO. The Romantic Agony. Translated by Angus David-
      son. London: Oxford Univ. Press, pp. 135, 179, 191, 296,
      305-08, 310, 317, 319-26, 361, 365-67, 383, 388, 394,
      404-405, 410, 416-18, 421, 425, 427-28, 430, 448.
        Reprint of 1933.5 in a slightly revised edition.

17 REISING, ROBERT W. "Huysmans' Against Nature and Eça de
      Queroz's The City and the Mountain: A Comparative Study."
      Language Quarterly, 9 (Fall-Winter), 37-40.
        Compares the heroes of both novels to refute Robert
      Baldick's assertion in the introduction to his translation
      of A Rebours (see 1959.1) that Jacinto imitates Des Es-
      seintes in most respects. "To argue that Jacinto is a
      virtual replica of Des Esseintes is to misunderstand one or
      both of the novels as well as to suggest that Eça de Queroz
      was not an imaginative creative artist. . . ." Huysmans'
      novel may be "the more powerful, the more profound, and the
      more moving," but The City and the Mountain "embraces so-
      cial, moral, and philosophical views totally dissimilar
      from those to which Huysmans subscribed in 1884."

18 VENEROSO, JACLYN. "The Theme of Ennui in the Novels of Joris-
      Karl Huysmans from Marthe to L'Oblat." Master's thesis,
      Brown University.

1970

19 WATERS, HAROLD A. Paul Claudel. New York: Twayne, pp. 29,
    156.
        Some critics point out that Huysmans and Claudel were at
    Ligugé about the same time, but question if they actually
    met. As an entry in Claudel's Journal reveals, he met
    Huysmans "two or three times in the summer of 1900 at
    Ligugé when I wanted to become a Benedictine."

1971

1   BABCOCK, JAMES C. "Portrait of the Contemporary Era in Huys-
    mans' Fiction: Its Nature and Development." Doctoral dis-
    sertation, Vanderbilt University.

2   BROOKNER, ANITA. The Genius of the Future: Studies in French
    Art Criticism. London: Phaidon, pp. 147-67.
        [Contains chapters on Diderot, Stendhal, Zola, the Gon-
    courts, and Huysmans.] Huysmans wrote art criticism of
    both an amateur and a professional nature. His critiques
    are always interesting and exude a peculiarly strong flavor
    of his personality, but art historians may regret the fact
    that he failed to live up to his early critical brilliance.

3   CEVASCO, G. A. "A Rebours and Poe's Reputation in France."
    Romance Notes, 13 (Winter), pp. 255-61.
        Translations of Poe's stories appeared as early as 1845,
    but his works were largely ignored in France until Huys-
    mans, led to Poe through his admiration of Baudelaire and
    Mallarmé, spoke glowingly of him in A Rebours. After the
    publication of A Rebours, interest in Poe abounded; the
    earlier efforts of Mallarmé (whose reputation was also en-
    hanced by Huysmans' novel) and Baudelaire to popularize the
    American author had borne no such fruit. Poe's "initial,
    continuing, and immense reputation in French literature is
    attributable in great measure to A Rebours."

4   CEVASCO, G. A. "Des Esseintes' Library." American Book Col-
    lector, 21 (Spring), 7-11.
        In his sybaritic seclusion at Fontenay, Des Esseintes
    has a cherished collection of books, all beautifully
    printed and magnificently bound. His library is the most
    notable part of his chateau. One section of his book-
    shelves is lined exclusively with Latin works; the other,
    with French. A Rebours is such an important literary land-
    mark because Huysmans' comments on Des Esseintes' library
    not only "mirrored decadent ideas and aspirations," but
    also "revealed and consecrated a new and exciting litera-
    ture, the literature of Baudelaire, Verlaine, and Mallarmé."

5   CEVASCO, G. A. "Sound of Color, Taste of Music: Synaesthesia
    in J.-K. Huysmans' Symphony of Spirits." Humanitas [St.
    John's Univ., NY], 4 (Winter), 14-15.
        Deals with synaesthesia in general and Huysmans' use of
    this secondary, subjective sensation in A Rebours. Des
    Esseintes has a collection of liqueur casks set up in an
    apparatus he refers to as his "mouth organ." Each liqueur,
    according to his taste, corresponds with the sound of a
    particular musical instrument. In imbibing drops of the
    various liqueurs, he provides his palate with sensations
    analogous to those which music dispenses to the ear. Des
    Esseintes is able to "perform upon his tongue silent melo-
    dies and mute funeral marches; to hear inside his mouth
    crème-de-menthe solos and rum-and-vestro duets." But after
    having tasted music and muddled all his senses, he begins
    to suffer complicated hallucinations of sight and hearing,
    and even the sense of smell. A physician warns him to stop
    further synaesthetic experimenting; and so Des Esseintes
    has to forego his "mouth organ."

6   DYRNESS, WILLIAM A. Rouault: A Vision of Suffering and Sal-
    vation. Grand Rapids, Mich.: Eerdmans, pp. 64-66, 188-89.
        Huysmans' ideal of religious art led him to retire to
    Ligugé, a small Benedictine monastery near Poitiers; and it
    was here that Rouault and the author of En Route met in
    1901. A few years before, Huysmans had decided to estab-
    lish a small community of artists and writers "who could
    work out their faith unhampered by the temptations and
    snares of the big city [Paris]." Huysmans urged Rouault to
    join his community, but shortly thereafter the entire proj-
    ect had to be abandoned because a ban on religious communi-
    ties forced the Benedictines to abandon their monastery and
    Huysmans to return to Paris. Under the influence of Huys-
    mans, however, Rouault turned his attention toward the
    mystical and to religious art.

7   HEMMINGS, F. W. J. Culture and Society in France, 1848-1898.
    London: B. T. Batsford, pp. 216, 220, 226, 230, 231, 234,
    243-44.
        Discussion of A Rebours, whose hero "became the very
    prototype and image of the nineteenth-century decadent."
    Alludes to the novel's influence in England on Moore and
    Wilde. Covers Huysmans' intention "to break out of the
    straitjacket of naturalism." Huysmans wrote La-Bas to
    rescue the novel form from materialism; in its opening
    pages he spelled out what "a great many men of Huysmans'
    generation, anxious, questing, disappointed with the bitter
    fruits of positivism, must have been privately thinking."
    Quotes some of Huysmans' atrabilious statements; shortly

1971

after the erection of the Eiffel Tower, for example, he de-
nounced it violently, calling it, among other things, "a
solitary suppository riddled with holes."

8   JULLIAN, PHILIPPE. Dreamers of Decadence: Symbolist Painters
     of the 1890's. Translated by Robert Baldick. New York:
     Praeger, pp. 28, 30, 45, 47, 74, 88, 92-93, 99, 103, 104,
     108, 140, 170, 190, 234, 238, 242, 247.
          Huysmans paid tribute to Félicien Rops, Pierre Puvis de
     Chavannes, Gustave Moreau, Odilon Redon, and other painters
     of Symbolism and Decadence. Huysmans was one of the first
     to bring Redon to the attention of the general public. He
     did so in a passage in A Rebours. In gratitude, Redon sent
     Huysmans a lithograph depicting the hero of the novel,
     Des Esseintes.

9   LAMM, MARTIN. August Strindberg. Translated by Harry G.
     Carlson. New York: Benjamin Bloom, pp. 268, 269, 291,
     537.
          Though "not temperamentally akin to Huysmans," Strind-
     berg was influenced by him. In 1897, he read En Route and
     observed in his Ockulta dagbok [Occult Diary]: "It is
     striking how his [Huysmans'] development progresses like
     mine. From magic and Satanism to Catholicism." During his
     final years, Strindberg was not so hostile to French sym-
     bolism as he pretended to be. He had read Baudelaire and
     Villiers de l'Isle-Adam with admiration, and "assimilated
     from Huysmans' later works the demands of the symbolists.
     . . ."

10   LIGHT, JAMES F. Nathanael West: An Interpretative Study.
     Evanston, Ill.: Northwestern Univ. Press, p. 59.
          Of particular importance in an understanding of The
     Dream Life of Balso Snell is Cabell's Jurgen and Huysmans'
     Là-Bas and En Route; from the former, West took aspects of
     his mannered tone and his questing plot; and from the lat-
     ter, he "gained a familiarity with mysticism."

11   MEIER, PAUL. "Circular Structure of A Rebours." Doctoral
     dissertation, Western Reserve University.

12   MILNER, JOHN. Symbolists and Decadents. New York: E. P.
     Dutton; London: Studio Vista, pp. 8, 33-34, 37, 42-47, 54,
     72.
          Much of A Rebours is taken up with elaborate descrip-
     tions of the fruit of Des Esseintes' hypersensitive taste;
     he came to exemplify "the model decadent aesthete." Moreau
     was one artist who excited Des Esseintes' "morbid imagina-
     tion"; Redon and Bresdin were others. Another Symbolist

painter that Huysmans admired was Pierre Puvis de Chavannes, about whom he wrote in one of his Salon reviews of 1883.

13 NELSON, JAMES G. The Early Nineties: A View from the Bodley Head. Cambridge, Mass.: Harvard Univ. Press, pp. 210, 218.
    Wilde's The Sphinx took its origins from an incident in A Rebours. In Le Gallienne's poem "The Decadent to His Soul," the protagonist exults like Huysmans' Des Esseintes over strange flowers he beholds.

14 O'BRIEN, JUSTIN. Contemporary French Literature. New Bruns-wick, N.J.: Rutgers Univ. Press, pp. 43-44, 47, 246.
    Correspondence between several sensations and a succes-sion of vivid remembrances in A Vau-l'Eau were appreciated by Proust. Cocteau was especially enamoured of Des Es-seintes and Dorian Gray.

15 POTEET, LEWIS T. "Dorian Gray and the Gothic Novel." Modern Fiction Studies, 17 (Summer), 239-48.
    Argues Wilde's debt to Huysmans' A Rebours is probably less than most critics contend. The direct influences are "pretty much limited to Chapters X and XI." Behind the larger scheme of Dorian Gray "lies a native, English Ro-mantic literary tradition, that of the Gothic novel."

16 RICHARDSON, JOANNA. Verlaine. New York: Viking, pp. 185-86, 198, 217, 236, 250, 287, 293, 299, 348, 356.
    When Huysmans first met Verlaine in 1884, he found him "a fascinating character--a combination of a brutal wheed-ling pederast and a confirmed drunkard. During the years that followed, Huysmans admonished the pederast and the drunkard, but helped the poet." They had a mutual admira-tion for one another's work. At one period in his life, Verlaine was haunted by Là-Bas: "I can't stop thinking about the people in Huysmans' novel Là-Bas."

17 SCHIFF, HILDA. "Notes Toward an Inquiry into Late Nineteenth-Century Literary Decadence." Anglo-Welsh Review, 19 (Spring), 91-96.
    Huysmans' A Rebours became the popular model for the mood; and with this novel the term decadent became the fa-vored catchword of the literati. If the salient features of the literature of the twentieth century have been dis-illusionment, cynicism, and negation, its origins must be sought in the decadence of the eighties and nineties in order to revaluate the spirit which prompted it.

1971

18 SHRAPNEL, NORMAN. "Varieties of Decadence." <u>Manchester</u>
    <u>Guardian</u> (11 March), p. 7.
        Huysmans was "an intensely visual writer, with eyes
    turned inward into the jewelled cave of his skull." <u>A Re-</u>
    <u>bours</u> is "a strange, heavily overseasoned novel," involved
    both with aesthetic antics and spiritual restlessness.

19 STARKIE, ENID. <u>From Gautier to Eliot: The Influence of</u>
    <u>France on English Literature, 1851-1939</u>. St. Clair Shores,
    Mich.: Scholarly Press, pp. 82-85.
        Reprint of 1960.8.

20 VIZETELLY, ERNEST ALFRED. <u>Emile Zola: Novelist and Reformer</u>.
    Freeport, N.Y.: Books for Libraries Press, pp. 146, 162-63,
    191, 207, 377.
        Reprint of 1904.5.

21 WATSON, HAROLD. <u>Claudel's Immortal Heroes: A Choice of</u>
    <u>Deaths</u>. New Brunswick, N.J.: Rutgers Univ. Press,
    pp. 107, 175.
        Claudel encountered the doctrine of vicarious suffering
    in the works of several writers, especially Huysmans,
    though Claudel denied that <u>Sainte Lydwine de Schiedam</u> was
    a direct influence. In 1915, Claudel "quoted copiously
    from Huysmans' annotated copy of St. Teresa of Avila's
    <u>Life</u> in his <u>Journals</u>."

22 WERNER, ALFRED. "Odilon Redon." <u>Art and Artists</u>, 6 (July),
    14-18.
        For Huysmans, Redon's work was "the nightmare trans-
    ported into art," and he never tired of praising "the
    bizarre talent of this singular artist."

23 WEST, T. G. "Schopenhauer, Huysmans and French Naturalism."
    <u>Journal of European Studies</u>, 1 (December), 313-24.
        Huysmans was attracted to Schopenhauer's pessimism. In
    the seventh chapter of <u>A Rebours</u>, Des Esseintes ponders the
    philosophy and compares it with that found in the <u>Imitation</u>
    <u>of Christ</u>; he finds in both certain qualities that help to
    appease his troubled existence. Schopenhauer's two basic
    remedies in life lay in art and in self-denial, "neither of
    which Huysmans understood with any depth." Christianity,
    as apprehended by Des Esseintes, also had its art and self-
    denial; and for those who accepted its tenets it promised
    spiritual consolation and hopes for an after-life.

Writings About Huysmans

1   BOROWITZ, HELEN O. "Visions of Salomé." Criticism, 14
       (Winter), 12-21.
            The power of the femme fatale which haunted the decadent
       hero is best told by Huysmans in A Rebours when Des Es-
       seintes contemplates Moreau's "Salomé Dancing Before Herod"
       and his "Apparition." Later, the legend is used by Wilde
       and Strauss and by Beardsley and Massenet.

2   CEVASCO, G. A. Oscar Wilde: British Author, Poet and Wit.
       Charlotteville, NY: Samhar Press, pp. 18-19.
            There is no record of Wilde's ever having met Huysmans,
       but it may be that from A Rebours Wilde first conceived the
       notion of writing a similar novel. For Wilde, Decadence
       became a fascinating religion, and like a Des Esseintes,
       Wilde sought for pleasures beyond the bounds of common
       approval.

3   CHARLTON, D. G., ed. France: A Companion to French Studies.
       London: Methuen, pp. 270, 274, 278, 349, 387, 388, 522.
            After being an admirer of Zola, Huysmans wrote A Re-
       bours, in which he evokes "the emptiness of an Epicurean
       search for novel sensations." In his later works of fic-
       tion, especially En Route, "he elaborates on the primarily
       personal and aesthetic reasons underlying his conversion."

4   FINKE, ULRICH. French Nineteenth-Century Painting and Litera-
       ture. New York: Harper & Row, pp. 193, 197, 200, 205-209,
       241, 243, 245, 289-91.
            Croquis parisiens contains examples of Huysmans' debt to
       Degas: "he sees the dancers at the Folies-Bergère exactly
       as Degas' ballet pictures, about which he had already writ-
       ten perceptively in 1876." Huysmans had installed one of
       Degas' ballet pictures in a place of honor in his apartment
       and wrote about it in En Ménage. Both Degas and Huysmans
       had a fascination for the ballet, the circus, the brothel;
       the latter, Degas captured in several monotones and Huys-
       mans wrote about in Marthe. Huysmans also admired Moreau
       and wrote at length of his "Apparition" in A Rebours, which
       contains, in addition, words of praise for another favorite
       artist, Redon.

5   GRANT, RICHARD B. The Goncourt Brothers. New York: Twayne,
       pp. 64, 128, 146, 153, 157.
            The Goncourts strongly influenced Huysmans during his
       early years as a writer. Their idea that "man can replace
       nature itself . . . prefigures Huysmans' A Rebours, the
       masterpiece of French literature that was to appear in

1972

1884." In A Rebours, Des Esseintes notes that he likes the Goncourts' literary style because it acts as an irritant to his jaded personality.

6   HOUSTON, JOHN PORTER. Fictional Technique in France, 1802-1927. Baton Rouge: Louisiana State Univ. Press, pp. 75, 76, 95-96, 101.

Unlike Zola, but like Edmond de Goncourt, Huysmans had little interest in plot structure: "all his efforts went into his elaborate style." While absorbing material associated with poetry, A Rebours "in chapter structure, stylistic polish, and consistent handling of point of view . . . remains in the realist-naturalist tradition." In his later novels, Huysmans abandoned the conventions of fiction for the essay form.

7   LUCIE-SMITH, EDWARD. Symbolist Art. London: Thames & Hudson; New York: Praeger, pp. 51, 54, 64-65, 67, 71-72, 74, 82, 84-85, 110, 140, 173-74, 198.

Any discussion of literary Symbolism cannot ignore the notion of Decadence "so powerfully exemplified in A Rebours and . . . Là-Bas." As a writer and a critic, Huysmans did a great deal to foster the Symbolist Movement in art.

8   McGUIRE, JOHN V. "Pilgrimage." Perpetual Help World (Summer), pp. 10-12.

At one time, Huysmans thought he found a haven in the person of Zola; but Zola was not a reasonable answer. During a pilgrimage, Huysmans devoted himself to medieval art, plain chant, liturgy, and mysticism. Only later did he come to look upon all such study "as the outward trappings of God's grace working quietly within him." He acknowledged this grace in three novels, En Route, La Cathédrale, and L'Oblat.

9   REWALD, JOHN, ed. Camille Pissarro: Letters to His Son Lucien. Mamaroneck, N.Y.: Paul P. Appel, pp. 31, 73, 114-15, 320, 321.

In a letter of May 9, 1883, Pissarro notes that he read Huysmans' L'Art moderne "with extreme interest," and that in the book Huysmans had been "exceedingly kind" to him. Letter dated March 1886 states that Pissarro had a long talk with Huysmans, who is "very conversant with the new art and is anxious to break a lance for us." Letter of June 4, 1887 comments that "Huysmans is more or less sympathetic to me; he understands what we are getting at. . . ." Letter of January 27, 1898 discusses the Dreyfus case and Huysmans' reactions to it. Letter of January 31, 1898 complains that Huysmans has entered "the religious fold. . . . Another invalid!" Letter of February 10, 1898 repeats gossip that Huysmans had not taken religious orders, that "he had found an interesting mine to exploit."

10   ROBBINS, AILEEN. "Tristan Tzara's Handkerchief of Clouds." Drama Review, 16 (December), 110-29.
        Mouchoir de Nuages [Handkerchief of Clouds] by Tristan Tzara has an easily discernible plot, based on a love-triangle, that is a slight parody of Là-Bas.

11   SPENCER, ROBIN. The Aesthetic Movement: Theory and Practice. London: Studio Vista; New York: E. P. Dutton, p. 140.
        Huysmans was an admirer of Randolph Caldecott's art and mentions him, along with Kate Greenaway and Walter Crane, in his Salon Review for 1881. These artists depicted "nostalgic images of old England which Des Esseintes was so eager to experience as the hero of Huysmans' fin-de-siècle novel A Rebours."

12   STEEGMULLER, FRANCIS. Maupassant: A Lion in the Path. Freeport, N.Y.: Books for Libraries Press, pp. 64, 98-117, 130, 137, 148-49, 171-72.
        Reprint of 1949.6.

13   TAYLOR, JOHN. "Joris-Karl Huysmans as Impressionist in Prose." Papers on Language and Literature, 8 (Fall), 67-74.
        Huysmans' advocacy of Impressionist painting had an effect on the development of his own fiction. A Rebours serves as an example of this innovative style and his technique of subordinating the experience of external reality to that of inner, spiritual reality. When he progressed from the anti-naturalism of style that A Rebours exemplifies to the anti-naturalism exemplified in Là-Bas, he expressed the change through impressionistic, psychological realism. Catholicism provided an answer to his spiritual crisis; Impressionism to matters of literary style.

1973

1   BERGONZI, BERNARD. The Turn of the Century: Essays on Victorian and Modern Literature. London: Macmillan; New York: Barnes & Noble, pp. 17, 25.
        Wilde's The Picture of Dorian Gray is "a pale imitation of Huysmans' A Rebours."

1973

2   BIRKETT, JENNIFER. "Huysmans." <u>Modern Language Review</u>, 68
    (July), 661-62.
        Review of M. Issacharoff's <u>J.-K. Huysmans devant la cri-</u>
    <u>tique en France, 1874-1960</u> (Paris: Klincksieck, 1970).
    The book has a relevance for Huysmans studies and contrib-
    utes at the same time to the general history of taste and
    ideas. Some chapters may be inadequate, but the volume
    does contain a large amount of complicated and detailed ma-
    terial which is efficiently and clearly analyzed and ar-
    ranged. The chapter on <u>En Route</u> is the best; it is "an
    exhaustive study on a variety of levels and proves an ex-
    cellent method for situating Huysmans' book in the contem-
    porary context."

3   CARTER, A. E. "J.-K. Huysmans and the Middle Ages," in <u>Medi-</u>
    <u>eval Studies in Honor of Robert White Linker</u>. Edited by
    Brian Dutton. Valencia, Spain: Castalia, pp. 17-53.
        As a young writer, Huysmans had a keen relish for con-
    temporary civilization and used it as the basis of his
    novels; yet he disliked the industrialism which made it
    possible. Later, he renounced the modern in favor of the
    medieval. His cult of the Middle Ages was only partially
    dependent on his conversion: "the cult came first and con-
    version second." At times, his medievalism was more anti-
    modern. His enthusiasm for the Middle Ages, however, is
    evident in <u>Là-Bas</u>, <u>La Cathédrale</u>, <u>Sainte Lydwine de Schie-</u>
    <u>dam</u>, and <u>Trois Eglises et Trois Primitifs</u>.

4   CEVASCO, G. A. "Des Esseintes' Tortoise." <u>Quartet</u> [Univ. of
    Texas], 6 (Winter), 11. [Translated into French by Mariska
    and John Sandiford-Pellé and published in <u>Bulletin de la</u>
    <u>Société J.-K. Huysmans</u> (Paris), no. 61 (46 Année), 13-14.]
        Original poem based on an episode in Chapter IV of <u>A Re-</u>
    <u>bours</u>, wherein Des Esseintes obtains a giant tortoise,
    glazes its carapace with gold and bedecks it with precious
    gems.

5   DAKYNS, JANINE R. <u>The Middle Ages in French Literature, 1851-</u>
    <u>1900</u>. London: Oxford Univ. Press, pp. xiii, xiv, 59, 215,
    217-18, 224, 230, 232-35, 236, 241, 244, 245-46, 252, 253,
    265, 266, 273, 279, 283, 291.
        Des Esseintes is drawn to medieval faith and art in
    <u>A Rebours</u>. In <u>Là-Bas</u>, Durtal is captivated by all aspects
    of the Middle Ages; in <u>En Route</u>, <u>La Cathédrale</u>, and <u>L'Oblat</u>
    he glories in it. Completely medieval in spirit, Huysmans
    despised "the watered-down religion of his day" and desired
    to see "the ferocious Catholicism of the Middle Ages re-
    stored to its full vigour."

6   FOWLIE, WALLACE. <u>French Literature, Its History and Its Mean-</u>
      <u>ing</u>. Englewood Cliffs, NJ: Prentice-Hall, pp. 180-181,
      184, 199, 204, 206, 208, 211-212.
          <u>A Rebours</u> "developed the theme of decadence in art." It
      created a sensation when first published in 1884 and formed
      "the basis for attitudes . . . referred to as aesthetic and
      decadent . . . that were struck in the nineties in France
      and in England." <u>Là-Bas</u> developed "themes of diabolism and
      black magic." <u>La Cathédrale</u> and <u>L'Oblat</u> "testify to Huys-
      mans' interest in Christian mysticism and medieval art."

7   FOWLIE, WALLACE. <u>Lautréamont</u>. New York: Twayne, pp. 45, 88,
      107, 115-16, 117, 118, 121, 126.
          Baudelaire's poems and Lautréamont's cantos prepared the
      way for <u>fin-de-siècle</u> books, especially <u>A Rebours</u>. In the
      domain of literary aestheticism, Lautréamont's <u>Les Chants</u>
      holds a position similar to that held by <u>A Rebours</u>: "both
      works . . . now seem to be works of pure revolt, not aber-
      rations, but vigorous renewals of strength."

8   FURST, L. R. "The Structure of Romantic Agony." <u>Comparative</u>
      <u>Literature Studies</u>, 10 (June), 125-38.
          The relationship between the Romantic Movement of the
      early nineteenth century and the so-called Decadence can be
      approached through a comparative analysis of Novalis' <u>Hein-</u>
      <u>rich von Ofterdingen</u> and Huysmans' <u>A Rebours</u>. The works
      are linked by numerous structural and thematic parallel-
      isms; but within these similarities there are deep diver-
      gencies "which suggest that Romantic Agony was an inversion
      of romantic idealism."

9   KENNEDY, VERONICA M. S. "Was Donald E. Westland Influenced by
      Joris-Karl Huysmans?" <u>Armchair Detective</u>, 6 (February),
      127-28.
          Did Westland in his detective novel <u>Bank Shot</u> (New York:
      Simon & Shuster, 1972) consciously or unconsciously parody
      Des Esseintes' macabre feast, as related in the first chap-
      ter of <u>A Rebours</u>, in the dinner party of Herman X, the
      Black Militant? "At any rate, it is refreshing to see how
      the Old Decadence of the Nineteenth Century perhaps adds a
      new dimension of humor to the crime novel of the Twentieth
      Century."

10   ROSSMAN, E. "The Conflict over Food in the Works of Joris-
      Karl Huysmans." <u>Nineteenth Century French Studies</u>, 2
      (Fall-Winter), 61-67.
          The subject of food is one that Huysmans utilized, per-
      haps unconsciously, in most of his works. He was both

1973

deeply attracted to and repelled by food and eating. This
culinary tension reveals several interesting things: first,
"food is one more element which links Huysmans to the intellectual concerns of our time"; second, despite his deep
and sincere involvement in religious art and the liturgy,
he remains "fundamentally a young savage with the most
literal-minded, naturalistic approach to religion"; third,
we are better able "to situate Huysmans in his revolt
against his time--the 'Banquet Years--which is our own
time"; and, finally, in his often disgusting descriptions
of gluttony he "lays bare the mindless, savage aggressive-
ness of any society of consumption."

11 RUDORFF, RAYMOND. The Belle Epoque: Paris in the Nineties.
New York: Saturday Review Press, pp. 40, 60, 66, 170,
194-98, 215-16, 218, 220-24, 228-29, 232, 238, 261, 263.
    Huysmans is discussed as one of the leading literary
personalities of the period. His A Rebours "popularized
the notion of the aesthete who . . . turns his back on the
ordinary world to plunge into new realms of sensory experience"; it encourages the public to think of "the 'modern'
poet or artist as a social eccentric with deplorable mor-
als." Huysmans' novel probably encouraged Rachilde to
write her notorious Monsieur Vénus. As for Là-Bas, it
popularized satanic rituals. Huysmans' essays on the Impressionists called attention to this revolutionary art
movement; he especially favored Cézanne and wrote about him
in Certains.

12 SWENSON, J. E. "Joris-Karl Huysmans: The Material Structure
of a Spiritual Aesthetic." Doctoral Dissertation, University of Virginia.

13 SYMONS, ARTHUR. "The Later Huysmans," in his Collected Works.
New York: AMS Press, pp. 187-97.
        Reprint of 1908.2.

1974

1 ATHERTON, JAMES S. The Books at the Wake: A Study of Literary Allusions in James Joyce's Finnegan's Wake. Mamaroneck,
N.Y.: Paul P. Appel, pp. 50, 258.
    Joyce used A Rebours as "a source book." The Wake has
an allusion to the dinner entirely in black described in
A Rebours, as well as a play upon the title of La Cathédrale.

126

1974

2   BALDICK, ROBERT. "Huysmans, Joris-Karl," in Collier's Ency-
       clopedia. Vol. XII. New York: Macmillan Educational
       Corp., 419-20.
          Biographical entry. "Huysmans' novels faithfully re-
       flect the development of the French intellectual and
       artistic life in the late nineteenth century."

3   CLOUGH, RAYMOND J. "The Metal Gods: A Study of the Historic
       and Mythic Aspects of the Machine Age in French Prose from
       1750 to 1940 [Zola, Huysmans, Proust, Verne, etc.]." Doc-
       toral dissertation, State University of New York at Buffalo.

4   DIJKSTRA, BRAM. "The Androgyne in Nineteenth-Century Art and
       Literature." Comparative Literature, 26 (Winter), 62-73.
          During the last two decades of the nineteenth century,
       androgynes appear with startling regularity in the work of
       the more unconventional artists and writers, especially
       among those whom Huysmans saw "as exponents of the revolt
       against the ascendancy of bourgeois values."

5   FRIEDMAN, MELVIN J. "The Symbolis Novel: Huysmans to Mal-
       raux," in Modernism: 1890-1930. Edited by Malcolm Brad-
       bury and James McFarlane. Harmondsworth, Middlesex:
       Penguin, pp. 453-66, 622.
          Huysmans, "a perceptive critic of Impressionistic art,"
       opened up "a deeply flanking movement out of orthodox na-
       turalism with his novels A Rebours . . . and Là-Bas."
       A Rebours has claims to being the first Symbolist novel;
       further, it is "a conspicuously verbal work . . . written
       by a man very much in love with language, who enjoyed in-
       dulging himself in rhetorical flourishes . . . in the
       sounds and contours of his words."
          Reprinted: 1976.4; 1978.4.

6   HEMMING, F. W. J. "Joris-Karl Huysmans," in his The Age of
       Realism. Baltimore: Penguin, pp. 200-207.
          Recounts the facts of Huysmans' life and discusses his
       works. Chief focus is on the novels of his naturalist
       phase, Marthe, Les Soeurs Vatard, En Ménage, and A Vau-
       l'Eau. Points out that in 1876, Huysmans' ideas were close
       to those of Zola, but that some eight years later he turned
       against the Naturalist novel, believing that Zola's brand
       of realism led only to "a spiritual bankruptcy." A Rebours
       ushered in a new kind of literature, that of aestheticism,
       decadentism, symbolism.

1974

7   LOWRIE, JOYCE O. "Joris-Karl Huysmans: From Satanism to
    Mysticism," in her The Violent Mystique: Thematics of
    Retribution and Expiation in Balzac, Barbey d'Aurevilly,
    Bloy, and Huysmans. Genève: Librarie Droz, pp. 131-55.
        The image of Satan underwent modifications in the pro-
    gression of ideas from Balzac to Huysmans. Satan's pres-
    ence "was felt acutely by Bloy and even more so by Huys-
    mans"; yet in En Route, Huysmans "shows that grace and
    forgiveness are possible after man's dark night of the
    soul." In tracing the development of the violent mystique
    from Balzac to Huysmans, one can find that the most impor-
    tant shift is one in emphasis: "while the depictions of
    man's violence remain fairly constant throughout, the
    elaboration of retribution and expiation move from a pe-
    ripheral to a central location."

8   MEYERS, JEFFREY. "Huysmans and Gustave Moreau." Apollo, 99
    (January), 39-44.
        Huysmans wrote on Moreau's art in Certains, and in
    A Rebours he described in minute detail the artist's two
    masterpieces, "Salomé Dancing Before Herod" and "The Appa-
    rition." The canvases express the artificial, the syba-
    ritic, the voluptuous and the voyeuristic qualities that
    Des Esseintes admires. Like Baudelaire, Mallarmé, and
    Flaubert, Huysmans and Moreau were fascinated by the
    Salomé theme. The sensual daughter of Herodias symbolized
    for Huysmans and Moreau a form of sexual abnormality and
    evil beauty. Their weird fascination with the "bored and
    fantastic woman, animal by nature," led Wilde to write his
    play Salomé in 1894; it was illustrated by Beardsley and
    transferred into an opera by Strauss in 1905.
        Reprinted: 1975.9.

9   NASSER, CHRISTOPHER S. Into the Demon Universe: A Literary
    Exploration of Oscar Wilde. New Haven, Conn.: Yale Univ.
    Press, pp. 55, 65, 93.
        The two major influences on the English Decadent Move-
    ment were Pater's Renaissance and Huysmans' A Rebours.
    Chapter XI of The Picture of Dorian Gray reflects A Re-
    bours, but there are strong echoes of The Renaissance in
    earlier chapters. Wilde's Salomé was also influenced by
    Huysmans: "The Salomé passages in A Rebours were at least
    partly responsible for firing Wilde's imagination to create
    his masterpiece of the Decadent Movement."

10   NUCCITELLI, ANGELA. "A Rebours' Symbol of the 'Femme-Fleur':
     A Key to Des Esseintes' Obsession." Symposium, 28 (Win-
     ter), 336-45.
          Huysmans established the basis for his system of symbols
     in his "Notice" [Prologue] to A Rebours when he provided
     numerous indications of Des Esseintes' current state of
     mind. Especially interesting is Huysmans' symbolic use of
     colors, liqueurs, and flowers. The flowers represent Des
     Esseintes' fear of the threatening figure of the seductive
     woman. Isolated symbols become linked as suppressed ele-
     ments of a terrifying symbol, that of the "Femme-Fleur,"
     who initially is associated with physical illness or
     wounds, and soon becomes the frightening result of sup-
     pressed passion and the incarnation of terror itself.

11   SCOTT, WILDER P. "French Literature and the Theater of
     Rodolfo Usigli." Romance Notes, 26 (Autumn), 228-31.
          The Mexican playwright Usigli was repeatedly influenced
     by French authors. The character Captain Des Esseintes in
     his Un Navio Cargardo de . . . clearly indicates Usigli's
     familiarity with A Rebours. Like his literary predecessor,
     the Captain is caught in his small world of art which he
     has created for himself through his collecting of paint-
     ings, coins, and objets d'art; but he manages to transform
     his material world into a spiritual one.

12   STEPHAM, PHILIP. Paul Verlaine and the Decadence, 1882-1890.
     Manchester: Univ. of Manchester Press; Totowas, NJ:
     Rowman & Littlefield, pp. 9, 10, 13, 14-15, 33, 42, 45, 58,
     63-69, 70-72, 73, 74, 77-80, 92, 94, 95, 102, 113, 119,
     142, 144, 145, 155, 161, 163, 186, 196.
          Upon its publication in 1884, A Rebours had "a substan-
     tial and beneficial effect on the fortunes of Verlaine and
     the decadents." Among Des Esseintes' favorite poets are
     Mallarmé, Corbière, and Verlaine. Huysmans' analysis of
     Verlaine's poetry in the novel is "accurate and sensitive."

13   TIHANY, E. D. "Huysmans: The Novel as Compromise." Doctoral
     dissertation, Yale University.

14   WINNER, ANTHONY. "The Indigestible Reality: J.-K. Huysmans'
     Down Stream." Virginia Quarterly Review, 50 (Winter),
     39-50.
          Down Stream presents the bachelor clerk as an everyman
     deprived of the fullness of everyday life. Folatin's
     search for comfort was conceived against the backdrop of
     Huysmans' own day-to-day occupation as a goverment clerk.

1975

> "The story of Huysmans' alter ego is distinguished from
> other monotonous studies of mediocre beings by its self-
> conscious awareness of its own sterility."

1975

1   ALDINGTON, RICHARD. <u>A Passionate Prodigality: Letters to
    Alan Bird, 1949-1962</u>. Edited by Miriam J. Benkovitz. New
    York: New York Public Library and Readex Books, pp. 278-79.
       In a letter dated April 16, 1960 writes of his visit to
    Colmar, where he spent the morning with superb Grunewald
    paintings--"'discovered' if I mistake not, by Huysmans."

2   BALASHOV, V. P. "Huysmans, Charles-Marie-George," in <u>Great
    Soviet Encyclopedia</u>. 3rd ed. [Moscow: Sovetskaia En-
    tsiklopediia Publishing House, 1970.] Vol. VII. New York:
    Macmillan; London: Collier Macmillan, 562-63.
       Biographical entry. As a Romantic, Huysmans "was at
    odds with the reality of capitalist society; this is evi-
    dent in his stories." He wrote of the "Parisian lower
    classes" and "the pathology of philistine egoism." After
    entering upon "the path of spiritual naturalism," he turned
    to Catholicism in 1892.

3   BURNS, C. A. "Henry Céard: Two Unpublished Diaries of 1878."
    <u>Nottingham French Studies</u>, 14: 11-19.
       Entries chiefly concerned with Céard's friendships with
    Zola, Flaubert, Edmond de Goncourt, and Huysmans. One pas-
    sage alludes to Huysmans' early career as a writer; another,
    on the impartiality and disinterestedness Huysmans displayed
    as a Naturalist.

4   CEVASCO, G. A. "Satirical and Parodical Interpretations of
    J.-K. Huysmans' <u>A Rebours</u>." <u>Romance Notes</u>, 16 (Winter),
    278-82.
       When first published in 1884, <u>A Rebours</u> meant different
    things to different critics, but none of them called it sa-
    tirical or parodical. Since the novel was published during
    an early phase of Decadence and actually helped to crystal-
    lize the Movement, can it be a satire or parody of a liter-
    ary movement in a generative stage? That the novel is
    neither satire, nor parody, nor caricature can be demon-
    strated in three ways: the way the book was read by its
    first critics; the reception the book received from the so-
    called Decadents themselves; and Huysmans' own views ex-
    pressed after the novel's publication and confirmed some
    twenty years later.

5   ENGSTROM, ALFRED G.   "A Rebours, Huysmans and the Decadent
    Way," in Darkness and Light.   Romance Monograph no. 16,
    Univ. of Mississippi, pp. 84-106.
        Gives short history of decadence in French literature,
    and then shows how "Huysmans had played a significant role
    in bringing it about, much of which is mirrored in A Re-
    bours." Focuses on Des Esseintes and his manner of living
    in his chateau at Fontenay.   The aestheticism of Des Es-
    seintes "seems to reflect Huysmans' own thought and taste."
    It is well to keep one's tongue in cheek when reading about
    the interrelated episodes of the tortoise, the dentist, and
    the mouth organ; for the details and episodes, "beyond
    their artifice and brilliant exaggeration," are "sad and
    empty."

6   HUNEKER, JAMES G.   "The Pessimist's Progress: J.-K. Huysmans,"
    in his Egoists: A Book of Supermen.   New York: AMS Press,
    pp. 167-206.
        Reprint of 1907.13.

7   HYDE, H. MONTGOMERY.   Oscar Wilde.   New York: Farrar, Straus
    & Giroux, p. 212.
        Delineates that part of Wilde's trial when the prose-
    cutor for the Crown questioned Wilde about "the poisonous
    book" that Dorian Gray was given by Lord Wooton.   Wilde ad-
    mitted that the book he had in mind was A Rebours, but he
    protested that to be examined upon the work of another
    artist would be "an impertinence and a vulgarity."

8   KNAPP, BETTINA.   Maurice Maeterlinck.   Boston: Twayne,
    pp. 25-26.
        Huysmans introduced the works of the fourteenth-century
    Flemish mystic Jean Van Ruysbroeck to Maeterlinck.   In
    1891, when Maeterlinck translated the mystic's Adornment of
    Spiritual Marriage from Flemish to French, he inscribed his
    gratitude in a volume he presented to the author of A Re-
    bours.

9   MEYERS, JEFFREY.   "Gustave Moreau and Against Nature," in his
    Painting and the Novel.   Manchester: Manchester Univ.
    Press; New York: Barnes & Noble, pp. 84-95.
        Reprint of 1974.8.

10 PASCO, A. H.   "En Rade and the Symbolic Integration of Self."
    South Atlantic Bulletin, 40 (January), 66.
        Despite the neglect and condemnation En Rade has had
    from most critics, when read with "a knowledge of the tra-
    ditional symbolic systems suggested by the text," this

1975

> novel is revealed as "a highly integrated, masterful account of the protagonist's struggle to understand and dominate himself."

11   POWELL, S. ROBERT.   "The Renaissance and Cubist Conception of Space and Art in the Nineteenth-Century French Novel [Zola, Huysmans, etc.]."   Doctoral dissertation, Indiana University.

12   PUTNAM, SAMUEL.   Preface to his translation of A Vau-1'Eau. New York: Fertig, pp. ix-xvi.
>   Reprint of 1927.2.

13   ROSE, M. G.   "Decadent Prose: The Example of Salammbô." Nineteenth-Century French Studies, 3 (Spring), 213-23.
>   In A Rebours, Huysmans linked the Salomé of Moreau's literary painting and the Salammbô of Flaubert's painterly novel in a fictional definition of Decadence.

14   TENNANT, P. E.   Théophile Gautier.   London: Athlone Press, pp. 101, 138, 139, 140.
>   Huysmans was indebted to Gautier for the neurotic mannerisms of Des Esseintes and for concepts of decadence, of which Mademoiselle de Maupin is a compendium of such themes.

15   WEINREB, RUTH PLAUT.   "Structural Techniques in A Rebours." French Review, 49 (December), 222-23.
>   A Rebours is mainly concerned with two unrelated subjects, discussions of art and the life of Duc Jean Des Esseintes. The only structural balance emerges from Des Esseintes' move from Paris to Fontenay and his ultimate return to Paris; yet Huysmans controls the quality of his protagonist's presence through four devices: direct discourse; the "neutral subject"; the present tense; and use of adverbs. When he is the subject, Des Esseintes acts strictly in a grammatical role; Huysmans selects colorless verbs to associate him with various authors and works. The present tense is used only when the main character has temporarily disappeared and never when the author refers to him in the more conventional parts of the book. Memory and dreams fulfill an important and identical role consistent with the nature of the narrative; they replace action and reality. The novelty of A Rebours arises from the absence of characters and development, from the distortions of time and space, and from the exaggerated importance of dreams and memories as technical devices.

1   ARMSTRONG, JUDITH. <u>The Novel of Adultery</u>. London: Macmil-
      lan, pp. 65, 71, 113, 145-46, 150-53, 156, 160, 164.
          Discussion of the work of Huysmans, Maupassant, Troyat,
      and Zola concerned with marital infidelity. Provides an
      account of the legal, social, and religious attitudes to
      both marriage and adultery in France, England, America, and
      Russia in the last half of the nineteenth century through a
      study of major and minor works of fiction written in those
      countries during the period. Prominent among such novels
      in France is Huysmans' <u>En Ménage</u>, which proclaims that
      "life holds nothing worth idealising, that marriage and
      concubinage are the only alternatives available to what is
      merely a physical need with few psychological overtones,
      and that either of the two is worth putting up with for the
      sake of domestic convenience." <u>Madame Bovary</u>, <u>The Golden</u>
      <u>Bowl</u>, and <u>En Ménage</u> are three important novels treating of
      adultery that suggest "an order which appears worth justi-
      fying even to the twentieth-century of permissiveness."

2   BRERETON, GEOFFREY. <u>A Short History of French Literature</u>.
      Baltimore, MD: Penguin, pp. 128, 226, 228-29, 232.
          Reprint of 1954.7.

3   FRIED, FREDERICK. "Joris-Karl Huysmans: The Experience of
      Self in the Transformation of Images." Doctoral disserta-
      tion, Johns Hopkins University.

4   FRIEDMAN, MELVIN J. "The Symbolist Novel: Huysmans to Mal-
      raux," in <u>Modernism: 1890-1930</u>. Edited by Malcolm Brad-
      bury and James McFarlane. Harmondsworth, Middlesex:
      Penguin, pp. 453-66, 622.
          Reprint of 1974.5.

5   GLICKSBERG, CHARLES I. "The Unpolitical Writer," in his <u>The</u>
      <u>Literature of Commitment</u>. Lewisburg, PA: Buckness Univ.
      Press; London: Associated Univ. Presses, pp. 113-30.
          <u>A Rebours</u> is an example of non-political literature which
      shows that not all of life can be legitimately included
      under the rubric of politics. To dismiss this novel simply
      as representative of "a psychological trend expressive of
      capitalism in its final stage of dissolution" would be
      wrong. Huysmans demonstrates that "art inspires types of
      commitment that do not fall within the categories prescribed
      by the Marxist aesthetic."

1976

6   GREEN, MARTIN. <u>Children of the Sun: A Narrative of Decadence
    in England After 1918</u>. New York: Basic Books, pp. 125,
    139, 141.
        Focuses on the influential generation of young writers
    who, in the aftermath of World War I, cultivated concepts
    of the dandy, the rogue, the naive. They favored such
    French poets as Mallarmé, Rimbaud, Verlaine and such fic-
    tion writers as Proust, Huysmans, and Cocteau. They re-
    pudiated Protestantism, leaned toward Rome and ritual, and
    admired "the black romanticism of Huysmans." They had "an
    intense susceptibility" to <u>A Rebours</u>.

7   JACKSON, HOLBROOK. <u>The Eighteen Nineties: A Review of Art
    and Ideas at the Close of the Nineteenth Century</u>. Atlantic
    Highlands, N.J.: Humanities Press, pp. 28, 58, 61, 63,
    136, 223.
        Reprint of 1913.2.

8   KELLMAN, STEVEN G. "The Self-Begetting Novel." <u>Western Hu-
    manities Review</u>, 30 (Spring), 119-28.
        The self-begetting novel "projects the illusions of art
    creating itself." <u>A Rebours</u> is in this sub-genre of the
    modern novel; for its narrative revolves about the solitary
    Des Esseintes, who like the typical narrator in this kind
    of fiction, retires to an isolated estate in order to fab-
    ricate every single detail of his existence. Tension in
    the work is found between Huysmans' inclination toward
    Decadence and Zola's demands in Naturalism. <u>A Rebours</u> con-
    fronts the reader with both process and product, quest and
    goal.

9   KRONENBERGER, LOUIS. <u>Oscar Wilde</u>. Boston: Little, Brown,
    pp. 56, 102, 104.
        Early in his career as a writer, Wilde admired such
    French writers as Huysmans and Barbey d'Aurevilly among the
    living; among the dead, Balzac, Gautier, and Baudelaire.
    <u>A Rebours</u> entered into Wilde's writing of <u>Dorian Gray</u>:
    "The metamorphosis of Dorian's self . . . is very much due
    to his reading of a 'poisonous yellow book,' Huysmans'
    <u>A Rebours</u>."

10 KUHN, REINHARD. <u>The Demon of Noontide: Ennui in Western Lit-
    erature</u>. Princeton, NJ: Princeton Univ. Press, pp. 322-26,
    329, 332, 338, 373.
        Discussion of <u>A Vau-1'Eau</u> as "a minor masterpiece" in
    which the main character, Jean Folatin, "gives himself up
    totally to a Schopenhauerian pessimism." Alludes to the
    boredom Camus portrays in <u>The Stranger</u> as a "duplication

of similar scenes in Huysmans' A Vau-l'Eau." Relates Huysmans to Kierkegaard, for at the end of A Rebours the world-
weary Des Esseintes is faced with conversion or suicide:
"Huysmans opted for the former as had Soren Kierkegaard."

11 LEEFMANS, BERT. "The Meanest Flower and the Rage for Order."
    Romanic Review, 67 (November), 308-12.
        In an analysis of Mallarmé's "Prose pour des Esseintes,"
    it is noted that the poet chided Huysmans "in sybilline
    fashion for a perverse oversimplification, for a failure to
    understand that there is more to [his] poetry, and to life,
    than decadence can grasp."

12 LINDER, ANN P. "The Devil in the Garden: The Vision of Para-
    dise in European Romantic Literature [Huysmans, Proust]."
    Doctoral dissertation, Rutgers University.

13 MAGILL, FRANK N., ed. Masterplots. Revised edition. Enlge-
    wood Cliffs, NJ: Salem Press, pp. 62-64; 1627-1630.
        Plot summaries and critiques of A Rebours and Là-Bas.

14 MATTHEWS, J. H. Towards the Poetics of Surrealism. Syracuse,
    NY: Syracuse Univ. Press, pp. 26-35, 45, 81, 97-98.
        Huysmans' name recurred with unexpected frequency in the
    conversations and writings of André Breton, the so-called
    "Father of Surrealism." Breton especially admired Huysmans
    because "he shared with me that vibrant boredom which al-
    most every sight caused him." Then too, it was the Huys-
    mans of A Rebours and En Rade whom Breton placed on the
    same level as Baudelaire, Rimbaud, and Lautréamont in his
    second Manifeste du Surréalisme. Among all surrealists,
    Huysmans "commands respect . . . as an exceptionally per-
    spicacious art critic."

15 PAUL, KEGAN. "Translator's Note," in his translation of En
    Route. New York: Fertig, pp. x-xi.
        Reprint of 1896.10.

16 SEYMOUR-SMITH, MARTIN. "England and Modernism: A Climate of
    Warm Indifference." Bananas, no. 6 (Autumn/Winter),
    pp. 3-7.
        References to Decadence and a brief discussion of
    Là-Bas.

1976

17 SEYMOUR-SMITH, MARTIN. "Huysmans, Joris-Karl," in <u>Who's Who</u> <u>in Twentieth-Century Literature</u>. New York: Holt, Rinehart & Winston, p. 171.
    Bio-critical entry. Huysmans' importance lies in the fact that his fictional characters "consistently seek to alleviate their existential disappointment," which makes him "a more distinctly modern writer than Zola."

18 STRICKLAND, GEOFFREY. "Penal Fancies." <u>Times Literary Sup-</u> <u>plement</u>, no. 3888 (17 September), p. 1182.
    Review of Victor Brombert's <u>La Prison romantique</u> (Paris: José Corti, 1976). Focuses on the prison house in French literature. Traces an evolution from the intensely person- al preoccupation with imprisonment of the early Romantics to our modern "<u>univers concentration-naire</u>," offering scholarly guidance to the works of Stendhal, Hugo, Nerval, Baudelaire, Huysmans, Camus, and Sartre which deal with this obsession.

19 WIGGINS, LORE I. H. "The City of Paris in the Works of Joris- Karl Huysmans." Doctoral dissertation, University of Texas at Austin.

20 WILLIAMSON, RICHARD C. "Towards Silence: Themes and Tech- niques in the French Symbolist Novel, 1884-1896." Doctoral dissertation, Indiana University.

21 WISSING, PAULA ANN. "The Role of the Object in the Novels of Joris-Karl Huysmans." Doctoral dissertation, University of Chicago.

1977

1 BANDY, W. T. "Huysmans and Poe." <u>Romance Notes</u>, 17 (Spring), 270-71.
    Claims that the influence of <u>A Rebours</u> in the spread of Poe's reputation in France was slight. (Attempts to refute 1971.3.) Maintains that there were frequent translations of Poe into French before 1884, but does not say anything about the critical articles and countless allusions that followed the publication of Huysmans' novel.

2 CEVASCO, G. A. "Something Exquisite and Spiritous: J.-K. Huysmans and George Moore." <u>Research Studies</u>, 45 (Septem- ber), 147-59.
    Moore was one of the first English writers to discover the author of <u>A Rebours</u>. The novel struck him as one of

the most remarkable books he had ever read: "Too exotic
for the ordinary reader, it was fit only for the literary
gourmet." So enamored was he of Huysmans' novel "that
soon, consciously and unconsciously, he began to imitate
its style and borrow its themes." The hero of A Mere Accident is modeled after Des Esseintes. Moore envisioned his
Confessions as the English equivalent of A Rebours. Mike
Fletcher was manifestly inspired by Huysmans' novel. Moore
drifted away from his early adulation of Baudelaire, Zola,
and Poe, his worship of Flaubert and Tolstoy, but he never
disavowed his admiration of Huysmans. They met several
times in Paris. Both explored religious subjects in their
later works of fiction. Moore would not have been able to
explore the religious elements in his Evelyn Innes and Sister Teresa had he not been familiar with En Route and La
Cathédrale; but the influence Huysmans exerted upon Moore
was literary and aesthetic, not religious. Moore never
underwent a transformation of spirit similar to Huysmans'.

3   CHARTIER, ARMAND B. Barbey d'Aurevilly. Boston: Twayne,
      pp. 81, 92, 99, 137, 160-63, 166, 169.
        In A Rebours, Huysmans drew attention to Barbey d'Aure-
      villy's Un Prêtre marié, calling it a novel in which "magic
      was mixed with religion, occult learning with prayer. . . ."
      Both authors turned Catholic, but there was a considerable
      distance between Barbey's "largely Jansenistic religious
      views" and Huysmans' "esthetic Catholicism." Barbey had
      personal reasons for being pleased by A Rebours: "it ap-
      peared to justify his opinion of Naturalism as a dead-end;
      moreover, Huysmans had expressed in his work deep admira-
      tion for Un Prêtre marié and for Les Diaboliques." Addi-
      tionally, Barbey was sensitive to the despair and anguish
      suffered by Des Esseintes.

4   CRAIG, ALEC. The Banned Books of England and Other Countries:
      A Study of the Conception of Literary Obscenity. Westport,
      Conn.: Greenwood Press, pp. 58, 93, 183-84.
        Reprint of 1962.3.

5   CROSBY, HARRY. Shadows of the Sun: The Diaries of Harry
      Crosby. Edited by Edward Germain. Santa Barbara: Black
      Sparrow Press, pp. 112, 155.
        In an entry dated July 5, 1926, Crosby notes that he is
      anxious to begin reading A Rebours and La Cathédrale after
      reading Symons' chapters on Huysmans in The Symbolist Move-
      ment in Literature (see 1919.7). Alludes to Des Esseintes
      in an entry dated August 30, 1927; how like the hero of
      A Rebours, Crosby saw enough of Englishmen and things Brit-
      ish in Paris not to undertake a long journey to England.

1977

6   FRANKLIN, URSULA. "Mallarmean Affinities in an Early Valéry Prose Poem." <u>French Review</u>, 51 (December), 221-32.
    Valéry much admired Mallarmé and was heavily influenced by his poetry, but <u>A Rebours</u> was Valéry's "<u>bible et . . . livre de chevet</u>." He admired the novel for many reasons, one being its focus on the prose poem. <u>A Rebours</u> provided the literary setting and frame of Valéry's "<u>Une Chambre Conjectural</u>." Valéry dedicated another poem, "<u>Les Vieilles Ruelles</u>," to Huysmans.

7   GUSTAITIS, J. "J.-K. Huysmans and France's Catholic Revival." <u>America</u>, 136 (30 April), 394-96.
    Huysmans was "one of the strangest, but also one of the greatest writers" of the late nineteenth century. As a Naturalist, he was extreme; whatever disgusted the senses gave him inspiration. Later, he came to know Catholicism through its artistic heritage. Today he is "widely read and studied in France." The example of his remarkable life still inspires others.

8   HARTNETT, E. "J.-K. Huysmans: A Study in Decadence." <u>American Scholar</u>, 46 (Summer), 367-76.
    Huysmans' importance lies in the fact that he became "the foremost exponent of the Decadent school," that his <u>A Rebours</u> "became the center of a new literary development."

9   MEYERS, JEFFREY. <u>Homosexuality and Literature, 1890-1930</u>. London: Athlone Press; New York: McGill-Queens Univ. Press, pp. 20, 26-27, 43, 165.
    Wilde derived sexual and aesthetic associations from <u>A Rebours</u>. In his novel, Huysmans connected reality with bourgeois respectability and conventional morality, and equated art with imagination, refinement, sensuality and immoral love. In Huysmans' and Wilde's scale of values "homosexuality, which is anti-social and taboo, is related to art; and homosexuals surround themselves with rich and elaborate illusions to 'spiritualize the senses.'" There is no doubt that Wilde was an overt homosexual, though Huysmans' sexual orientation was "dubious." [In a letter to André Raffalovich that Huysmans wrote in 1904, thanking him for his treatise <u>Uranisme et Unisxualité</u>, he commented: "Your letter and your book bring back to mind some horrifying evenings I once spent in the sodomite world, to which I was introduced by a talented young man whose perversities are common knowledge. I spent only a few days with these people before it was discovered that I was not a true

homosexual--and then I was lucky to get away with my life. . . ." (Quoted by Robert Baldick in his Life of J.-K. Huysmans, p. 82; see 1955.3.)]

10 MONSMAN, GERALD. Walter Pater. Boston: Twayne, pp. 157, 169.
      Possibly Wilde at his trials would have cited Pater's Renaissance as Dorian's corrupting "golden book," but he chose instead Huysmans' A Rebours so as not to compromise Pater.

11 POPKIN, DEBRA and MICHAEL POPKIN, eds. "Huysmans, Joris-Karl," in Modern French Literature: A Library of Literary Criticism. Vol. I. New York: Ungar, 517-25.
      Excerpts from the works of such critics of Huysmans as Remy de Gourmont (see 1921.4), Havelock Ellis (see 1898.15), Paul Valéry (see 1968.12), Gilbert Highet (see 1957.4), Robert Baldick (see 1955.3), and George Ross Ridge (see 1968.8).

12 SHENTON, C. G. "A Vau-l'Eau: A Naturalistic Sotie." Modern Language Review, 72 (April), 300-309.
      A Vau-l'Eau, which grew out of Huysmans' feelings for the bizarre and grotesque, had its origin in a section of Croquis parisiens entitled "Fantaisies et petits coins." Here is found the source of "M. Folatin's ridiculous adventures among the eating houses of the Left Bank." The novel is "a comic demonstration, by a reduction to the absurd, of the axioms of Schopenhauerian pessimism."

1978

1 CAVE, RICHARD. A Study of the Novels of George Moore. New York: Barnes & Noble; Gerrards Cross, Buckinghamshire: Colin Smythe, pp. 102-105.
      Moore's excitement over A Rebours in 1884 was prompted not simply by the book itself but by the possibilities for future fiction that Huysmans had revealed. Huysmans' style, form, and content worked well enough for him, but for Moore it was an "initial and principal mistake." Because of his imitation of Huysmans, the characters in Moore's early novels were all "'trapped' both within their own mentalities and within Moore's fictional technique."

2 CEVASCO, G. A. "J.-K. Huysmans and Aubrey Beardsley." <u>Bulletin de la Société J.-K. Huysmans</u>, Tome XVI, no. 68, 11-25.
   Early in his career Beardsley focused his attention on Whistler, Wilde, and Huysmans. Huysmans' Des Esseintes especially appealed to the young artist, whose "Peacock Skirt" drawing is "a transmutation of Moreau's 'Salomé Dancing Before Herod' as experienced by Des Esseintes." Huysmans' influence can also be recognized in Beardsley's <u>Under the Hill</u>.

3 CEVASCO, G. A. "No Silver Thread: J.-K. Huysmans and Max Beerbohm." <u>Studies in the Humanities</u>, 7 (December), 28-31.
   To identify Beerbohm too closely with Huysmans would border on the hyperbolical; there was no silver thread between them. Nevertheless, during his twenties, when active as the Comic Genius of the Nineties, Beerbohm did write at times in the shadow of Des Esseintes.

4 FRIEDMAN, MELVIN J. "The Symbolist Novel: Huysmans to Malraux," in <u>Modernism: 1890-1930</u>. Edited by Malcolm Bradbury and James McFarlane. Hassocks, Sussex: Harvester Press; Atlantic Highlands, NJ: Humanities Press, pp. 453-66, 622.
   Reprint of 1974.5.

5 GIRAUD, RAYMOND. "Huysmans, Joris-Karl." <u>Encyclopedia Americana</u>. Vol. XIV. Danbury, Conn.: Americana Corp., 625.
   Biographical entry. A disciple of Zola, Huysmans wrote in "a rich, dense, tormented style." He is important "for his contribution to the 'decadent' movement and his portrayal of his conversion through satanism to Christianity."

6 GREAVES, ANTHONY A. <u>Maurice Barrès</u>. Boston: Twayne, pp. 13, 37, 43, 110.
   At an early date [1883], "Barrès was attracted to the work of Huysmans, . . . the outstanding representative of Decadentism and the <u>fin de siècle</u>." Later, he did not defy the present or yearn for the past as did Huysmans, especially as he did in <u>Là-Bas</u>.

Index

This index lists the names of all authors, Huysmans' editors and translators, and subjects that appear in Part II of this Reference Guide: "Writings About Huysmans in English, 1880-1978." All titles of works discussed in the annotations are also listed. Each listing carries a reference to year and entry number. A select group of subject headings pertaining to Huysmans' life and work can be found listed alphabetically under his name. The titles of his individual works are arranged in the sub-category under Huysmans "works by"; to facilitate use of this part of the index, additional sub-categories have been utilized, where appropriate, under the title of each work.

Index

Le B., F. P., 1923.10
Leefmans, Bert, 1976.11
Le Gallienne, Richard, 1896.9;
   1971.13
Legends (Strindberg), 1929.4
Lehmann, A. G., 1950.4
Letters, Francis J. H., 1948.7, 8
Lewis, Jack, 1921.4; 1967.9
Lhombreaud, Roger, 1964.3
Life of J.-K. Huysmans, The
   (Baldick), 1955.1-4, 7, 11,
   15-19, 22; 1956.2, 3, 5;
   1957.1; 1960.1; 1977.9
Liguge, Benedictine Monastery at,
   1901.1, 5; 1950.3; 1969.23;
   1970.19; 1971.6
Linder, Ann P., 1976.12
Littlefield, Dorothy A., 1942.2
Livre de la Route, Le
   (Jorgensen), 1928.3
Lobet, M., 1962.2
Lorrain, Jean, 1933.5
Louys, Pierre, 1962.3
Loving, Pierre, 1923.11
Lowrie, Joyce O., 1974.7
Lucie-Smith, Edward, 1972.7
Lueders, Edward, 1955.14

M., W. P., 1954.10
McAghon, Arthur D., 1935.4
MacCarthy, Desmond, 1935.5
McCarthy, Elizabeth, 1961.3
McCole, C. John, 1937.1
McDermott, T., 1945.1
McGill, V. J., 1965.7
McGuire, John V., 1972.8
MacIntyre, C. F., 1957.5; 1964.9
McKalik, Benjamin M., 1970.12
Mackenzie, Compton, 1965.4
MacLeish, Archibald, 1970.12
McMahon, J. H., 1925.3
Macy, John, 1961.4
Madame Bovary (Flaubert), 1976.1
Mademoiselle de Maupin
   (Gautier), 1933.5; 1975.14
Madsen, Borge Gedso, 1962.10
Maeterlinck, Maurice, 1893.2;
   1975.8
Magic Mountain, The (Mann, T.),
   1948.7

Magill, Frank N., 1956.10;
   1958.8; 1960.3; 1963.8;
   1964.4; 1965.3; 1968.7;
   1976.13
Mallarmé, Stéphane, 1893.2;
   1931.10; 1933.5; 1938.3;
   1939.1; 1950.4; 1951.3;
   1952.4; 1953.1; 1955.9;
   1957.5; 1960.10; 1964.7;
   1966.6, 8, 12, 15; 1968.4;
   1969.18; 1970.3; 1971.3;
   1974.8, 12; 1976.6, 11;
   1977.6
Manet, Edouard, 1949.4; 1961.8;
   1970.14
Manifeste du Surréalisme
   (Breton), 1976.14
Mann, Klaus, 1953.4
Mann, Thomas, 1948.7
Marchand, Henry L., 1933.3
Marten, Kurt, 1953.4
Martin, Elizabeth P., 1952.4
Mason, H. [T.], 1961.5; 1965.7
Massenet, Jules, 1972.1
Massie, Patricia, 1948.8
Master's theses [on Huysmans],
   1931.7, 9; 1940.2; 1942.2;
   1949.1; 1955.20; 1956.11;
   1961.3; 1966.15; 1970.13, 18.
   See Doctoral dissertations.
Matthews, J. H., 1964.5, 6;
   1966.16; 1976.14
Maupassant, Guy de, 1928.4;
   1932.1; 1949.6; 1953.7, 8;
   1954.13; 1959.10; 1966.9, 13;
   1972.12; 1976.1
Medievalism, 1924.11; 1973.3, 5
Meier, Paul, 1971.11
Mere Accident, A (Moore), 1934.3;
   1948.2; 1977.2
Merrill, Stuart, 1952.2
Merrit, James Douglas, 1969.17
Mespoulet, M., 1947.2
Meyer, Laura K., 1970.13
Meyers, Jeffrey, 1974.8; 1975.9;
   1977.9
Mike Fletcher (Moore), 1934.3;
   1976.2
Miller, Henry, 1952.5
Millet, Jean-François, 1969.11
Milner, John, 1971.12

Index

"Rosa Alchemica" (Yeats), 1959.2
Rose, M. G., 1975.13
Rosicrucianism, 1959.2
Rossman, E. D., 1969.19; 1973.10
Rothenstein, William, 1931.10
Rouault, Georges, 1971.6
Rouleau, Sister M. Celeste,
    1956.11
Rousseau, Jean Jacques, 1907.15
Rudorff, Raymond, 1973.11
Rudwin, J. J., 1920.5
Ruysbroeck, Jan Van, 1975.8
Ryland, Hobart, 1949.5

S., H., 1924.9
S., R., 1952.7
Sade, Marquis de, 1949.5
Saintsbury, George, 1919.6
Salmmbô (Flaubert), 1966.4;
    1975.13
Salomé (Wilde), 1974.8, 9
Salomé Theme, 1960.4, 10; 1972.1;
    1974.8; 1975.13
Saltus, Edgar, 1933.2; 1952.2;
    1968.11
Samuel Perkins: Smeller (West),
    1931.11
Sand, George, 1897.1; 1969.11
Sandiford-Pellé, J. W. G.,
    1969.20
Sartre, Jean-Paul, 1976.18
Satanism. See Diabolism.
Saurat, Dennis, 1946.5
Savoy, The, 1953.8
Schiff, Hilda, 1971.17
Schopenhauer, Arthur, 1953.2;
    1963.7; 1971.23; 1976.10;
    1977.12
Schwab, Arnold T., 1963.9
Scott, Wilder P., 1974.11
Senior, John, 1959.8
Sewell, Brocard, 1968.9
Seymour-Smith, Martin, 1976.16,
    17
Shapiro, Karl, 1968.10
Shenton, C. G., 1977.12
Sheppard, Lancelot C., 1955.18;
    1960.1, 6, 7; 1963.10
Shrapnel, Norman, 1971.18
Shroder, Maurice Z., 1961.10

Shuster, George, 1921.6
Sinister Street (Mackenzie),
    1965.4
Sisley, Alfred, 1970.14
Sister Teresa (Moore), 1947.3;
    1948.2; 1977.2
Sloane, Joseph C., 1941.1
Smith, A. C., 1930.4
Smith, Maxwell, 1938.4
Société J.-K. Huysmans, 1956.2;
    1965.5
Soirées de Medan, Les, 1928.4;
    1932.1; 1949.6; 1953.7;
    1966.7, 8
Sommer (Jorgensen), 1969.13
Spencer, Robin, 1972.11
Sphinx, The (Wilde), 1948.2;
    1971.13
Spiritual Naturalism, 1960.9;
    1965.4; 1975.2
Sprague, Claire, 1968.11
Starkie, Enid, 1954.11; 1955.2,
    19; 1960.8; 1971.19
Steegmuller, Francis, 1949.6;
    1972.12
Steinberg, S. H., 1954.12
Stendhal, 1976.18
Stepham, Philip, 1974.12
Steward, S. M., 1934.3
Stranger, The (Camus), 1976.10
Strauss, Richard, 1972.1; 1974.8
Strickland, Geoffrey, 1976.18
Strindberg, August, 1929.4;
    1962.10; 1965.7, 9; 1970.11;
    1971.9
"Studies in Strange Sins"
    (Symons), 1960.4
Sturm, Frank Pearce, 1969.21
Suetonius, 1956.8
Sullivan, Edward D., 1954.13
Summers, Montague, 1932.4;
    1946.6; 1948.9; 1965.5
Surrealism, 1962.8; 1964.5;
    1966.6, 16; 1976.14
Swart, Koenraad W., 1964.7
Swenson, J. E., 1973.12
Swift, Jonathan, 1917.3; 1952.8
Symbolism, 1938.3; 1951.3;
    1953.8; 1954.7; 1966.8, 12;
    1967.3, 15; 1971.8, 12;
    1972.7; 1974.6

Index